My Way
to Help You Live
with Someone Else's Anger

A Ten Step Guide

Lynda Bevan

PublishAmerica
Baltimore

First printing

The front cover art was painted by Welsh Artist Ms. Christine Eynon.

ISBN: 1-4241-1380-6
PUBLISHED BY PUBLISHAMERICA, LLLP
www.publishamerica.com
Baltimore

Printed in the United States of America

This book is dedicated to the memory of my parents and grandparents, in gratitude for the wonderful memories that are imprinted on my mind.

Contents

Introduction

I am going to start this book by saying that anger frightens me. I have seen anger too many times, during the course of my life, and it has terrified me! In this book I will try and explain, simply, which is the only way I know how to explain anything, what anger is, and ways you can adopt to attempt to defuse it. There is no magic key to dealing with anger—there is no simple solution!

I emphasise that the patients I refer to in this book, who have attended sessions with me, and who are experiencing anger at home, are not necessarily inadequate, ineffective individuals. On the contrary, some are professional, powerful people. The things that bind these patients together, and they all have in common, is that when they fell in love they gave their partner, not only their love but also their soul (in other words they gave their partner 100% of themselves). Also, none had thought that they had been the victims of slow mind control/brainwashing.

Where Does Anger Come From?

Anger is an emotion. It stems from issues in your past that are both unresolved and unforgiven! These feelings are buried deep down inside you and cause you emotional and physical harm.

Anger comes from a past environment of confusion, chaos and lack of communication between family members. If you have seen your parents become angry, on a regular basis, you will perceive this behaviour as normal and are more likely to adopt the same method of interaction yourself.

Anger is a habit that is rooted in our sub-conscious mind. It is a formed pattern of behaviour that is firmly established. A pattern of behaviour/habit can be changed. Anger is based in your own fear and insecurities and a belief that you are, or have been wronged.

Anger (healthy)

It is important to understand that there is a positive side to anger. Healthy anger is part of the basic belief system that stems from a 'high frustration tolerance level'. Anger used in its positive sense provides us with the drive to attempt and accomplish difficult tasks we perceive as threatening or unattainable/out of our reach. It motivates us to push ourselves that extra mile in order to achieve the unachievable! Positive anger is an essential element in our lives. Without it we are lethargic, hopeless, unmotivated and negative. Positive anger gives us the energy to tackle situations/obstacles/opportunities that are challenging. It allows us to expand our boundaries and take risks.

Healthy Anger Stems from a Set of Healthy Beliefs

Passion	Accountable	Competence
Drive	Honesty	Adequacy
Enthusiasm	Dependability	Intuition
Energy	Loyalty	Perception
Responsible	Lovable	Confident
Respectful	Equality	Assertive

Anger (Unhealthy)

Is part of the belief system that stems from a 'low frustration tolerance level'. Therefore, when faced with any situation that you are unable to understand or deal with, you resort to anger. When you resort to anger you are actively engaging in

MY WAY TO HELP YOU LIVE WITH SOMEONE ELSE'S ANGER

threatening and/or frightening people in order to push them away, and not engage in the conversation or set of circumstances that presents itself. You do this because you are unable to participate in healthy discussions that you cannot control.

Unhealthy Anger Stems from a Set of Unhealthy Beliefs

A need to control
A dislike of criticism
Resentment
Jealousy
Envy
Fear

Rejection
Failure
Intimacy
Incompetence
Inadequacy
Lack of education

Lethargy
Hopelessness
Unmotivated
Unintuitive
Unperceptive

Ten Steps on How You Use Unhealthy Anger

To get our own way
To sabotage ourselves and others
To frighten someone into submission
To control people, situations and outcomes
To shift blame from ourselves
To show disrespect
To criticise
To intimidate
To victimise
To bully

9

Step One:
To Get Our Own Way

This is wanting to and having total control. Putting yourself first at any price! Being selfish! This individual is frightened of what would happen if he/she didn't have total control. They are scared that, if they are not in control of all situations and people nearest to them, their circumstances/life could change dramatically and they would be left 'high and dry'. They have no basic self-respect or like themselves and believe they are not liked or respected by others and, therefore, they have a desperate need to stay in control in order to keep and preserve what they have. They feel they are failures!

They manipulate those people closest to them by any method that works for them by, i.e.:

—Menacing behaviour
—Coaxing and cajoling
—Luring you into a false sense of security
—Sulking
—Aggression
—Attacking
—Bribery
—Threatening
—Walking out (as if never to return—you wish!)—he/she will be
   back!

—Violence (as in slamming doors, stamping around the house)
—Body language (large and looming over you)
—Accusing
—Blaming
—Physical Violence (when this occurs, or if there is a strong probability of this happening in your relationship—GET OUT!)

In my opinion, this type of person is only respected by people who know them on a superficial level. This controlling type can be friendly, talkative and interesting in professional and social situations. It is only when someone oversteps the self-imposed boundaries of the controller that outsiders will spot that the person is intolerant, aggressive, rude and threatening.

Example: Some years ago I saw a patient who told me that his wife had forbidden him to visit his longstanding friend (he had been friends with this person for twenty years). The reason his wife had, initially, given was that she did not, personally, know his friend and had never been invited to visit him. She was angry and felt excluded from the relationship and, worse, accused him of having a homosexual relationship with his friend. She was very angry and aggressive whilst discussing this issue, which caused a major disruption in the household. Whilst my patient could accept the point his wife made regarding feeling excluded from the long-standing friendship, he could not, and would not, accept the accusation that he was conducting a homosexual affair with his friend. However, he discussed this issue with his friend and, despite the inexcusable remarks, an invitation was extended to her to 'call in any time' for a chat. This offer was unacceptable to my patient's wife who felt that she was being fobbed off as no *definite* invitation date had been extended. My patient continued to see his friend (once/twice a week) popping in for a coffee and a chat. It was a ridiculous situation and he felt guilty doing something without his wife's knowledge. However, he felt he needed to make a stand on this issue. On one occasion when he was visiting his friend, there was a knock at the door and his wife appeared on the doorstep. My patient's friend invited her into his home for a coffee but she refused and was very hostile, angry and rude. She had called into the friend's house on the pretence to tell her partner that she was going somewhere and would not return for a couple of hours. What she was actually doing was making her presence felt in the most threatening and intimidating manner. She left her husband in no doubt of the confrontation that was to follow later. She was, in other words, menacing him!

My patient was totally embarrassed and fearful of the outcome! He had experienced this behaviour many times, by his wife, and had always made excuses for her and accommodated her outbursts. He loved his wife and wanted a successful marriage but he also wanted to 'hang out' with his friend and be able to 'shoot the breeze', occasionally, as they had done prior to his marriage. It wasn't as if he went out for a drink with his friend and met other people he had previously known! This situation totally disabled him, describing his reaction to the event as feeling 'weak in the knees', having a dry mouth and unable to have a clear, logical thought in his head. He couldn't stay at the friend's house after this incident had occurred and left immediately following his wife in an attempt to offset the inevitable major argument that was to follow. This act of scurrying after his partner only added fuel to his partner's fire as the wife then knew that her behaviour had achieved its required result: to get her own way!

Negative Options on How to Deal with Someone Always 'Getting Their Own Way'

—Do anything you want behind your partner's back!
—Try and coax, cajole and beg your partner into agreeing with you.
—Tell the truth at all times (in the full knowledge that the outcome will be anger), and put up with the consequences
—Enter into lengthy discussions about the innocence of your intentions (usually to no avail)
—Give him/her support at any price

—Love him/her more, and dance to their tune, to show and prove you could never, or would not want to be, without them
—Give in and submit all the time
—Give up on having a life of your own
—Fight 'fire with fire' and retaliate with anger

Or...Positive Options on How to Deal with Someone Always 'Getting Their Own Way'

—Be still—do not react—let them 'run out of steam'
—Do not be provoked, whatever they say
—Stay in control of YOU
—Devise a plan of action (the outcome you want to achieve)
—Stay focused on what you want
—Say nothing, other than giving answers such as, "I am not responding to you because I don't know the answer yet, and can't give you the answer you want at this time."
—Continue (quietly and unobtrusively) to follow your own plan and do your own thing (this will give you confidence and raise your self-esteem)
—Encourage open and honest discussions during quiet, peaceful, relaxing times
—When there is an easy flow of conversation taking place between you, assess whether it might be an appropriate time to air an issue causing you concern, i.e. "when we argue I feel unable to respond to you because you shout and frighten me with your presence." This admission, gently said and repeated over many months, might eventually sink in and he/she might decide to start listening and stop shouting.
—Decide to change yourself (taking small steps and making small changes at first). This will provoke him to respond to you in a different way. If this is done slowly there will be a positive result as shown in my book, a 10 step-guide called *My Way to Help You Live in a Difficult Relationship*. This guide is an empowering strategy for change in relationships.
—Decide to leave him/her

Step Two: To Sabotage Ourselves and Others

People sabotage themselves in order to stay the same. They dare not take risks and change anything because that would mean that they would not be in control of their lives, homes and people. These people are also afraid of change. They stay the same to stay in control. Fundamental issues, such as moving house, new job opportunities, new friends, new social habitats, new hobbies, are all potential circumstances that would change their lives and might result in something being taken away from them. The risk is too big, therefore they opt to stay in the cocoon of their own making. Unfortunately when this happens they usually take prisoners with them who are also trapped in their cocoon. This cocoon stops the people they are close to from progressing and moving forward in their lives. Saboteurs are selfish and stuck in a rut of their own making. They cause the people who fall in love with them horrendous misery and unhappiness. When a saboteur/controller (angry person) has established himself/herself firmly within the family he/she will be reluctant and resistant to any change of circumstances. This is due to the saboteur/controller's inflexibility and uncompromising attitude and fear of losing his/her position in the family unit. Rules are established in the household, imposed by the saboteur/controller, and if these rules are broken, all hell breaks loose. These rules can be as inconsequential as, i.e., always ensuring that doors are closed behind you if you leave a room or staying out later in the evening without prior permission from the saboteur/controller. If these rules are broken, the consequence to the perpetrator is horrendous. Anger abounds in order to ensure that, in future, no rules are broken. I have heard patients who have, themselves, imposed these rules say that this is how to gain the respect they feel they deserve. Unfortunately, this is not so. This household is managed by fear and there is no respect!

Options on How to Deal with Someone Who Sabotages Himself/Herself as the Example Shows

—Ensure the rules of the household are agreed by all who live in the house
—Ensure the rules are realistic and appropriate
—Agree to allow some flexibility of the rules
—Agree that if a rule is broken, the issue will be discussed as a family unit and the person punished appropriately
—Agree that there will be a trial period for the rules imposed

Examples of Self-Sabotage

One patient, male, who I saw on a regular basis, told me that he needed to earn more money in order to sustain the standard of living in the household. He was a successful, clever guy with many skills. Unfortunately, as he explained, his financial position had remained the same over a given period of time and had not risen in line with the 'extras' both he and his partner enjoyed. He explored avenues of making extra money, i.e., finding a new job, starting up his own business. All the avenues he explored offered opportunities. There was the possibility of starting up his own business (with a colleague), also the opportunity of working in another country (for a limited period) with the prospect of excellent financial payoffs. However, after lengthy discussions with his partner, he opted to remain doing the same job he had always done for the same financial returns! This resulted in the family lowering their standard of living to accommodate this decision. Ultimately he was afraid of 'taking a risk' and changing his professional working pattern. He gave up and gave in! As a consequence to this decision, over a period of time, he became lethargic, unmotivated and lacking in self-respect.

One young girl came to see me at the Health Centre. She was very pretty, talented and articulate. However, she believed she was unattractive and useless. She repeatedly told herself, when looking in the mirror, how ugly she was and why would anyone want to be with her? Every job interview she attended the same pattern occurred: she asked herself, ' Why would she get the job?' This young lady was brainwashing herself into believing that nothing good was going to come her way. She was sabotaging herself! "If you believe you can't—you won't."

How to Deal with a Self-Saboteur
Negative Points

—Listen to his/her plans and take them with a 'pinch of salt'
—Don't believe everything they tell you
—Don't rely on the outcome they expect
—Always have a realistic Plan B (one that involves you!)
—Whilst being flexible, compromising and adaptable—don't be fooled into believing everything is going to be all right because they said so!
—If there is something you want (i.e. buy a house, buy a car, getting a job, changing the kid's school), make sure that you research the commodity, discuss and prepare all documentation thoroughly with professionals prior to presenting it to your partner. Introduce the subject gently and informally at first (getting them used to the idea). They will, initially, resist taking the risk. However, gentle persuasion and negotiating skills will win with perseverance.

Positive Points

—Give them encouragement and support whenever possible
—Reinforce their good points
—Try to keep them within realistic boundaries of their expectations of themselves
—When discussions arise, paraphrase (so that they can see that you understand the topic being discussed) and offer logical responses giving examples of the points you identify in order to reinforce, clarify and justify your conclusions, thereby allowing no error for misconception on their part of your opinions.
—Encourage this individual to set themselves small achievable targets and support them in obtaining a positive result.
—Support them in taking small, unimportant risks.
—Get them used to the idea of change in small, inconsequential ways.

Step Three: To Frighten Someone into Submission

When disagreements occur anger is used to get someone/his/her/partner to submit! The argument/discussion usually starts in a reasonable way but very soon spirals out of control. This happens when the controller sees that they could lose the argument and not get their own way. The voice rises, eyes bulge in the head, the face turns the colour of corpse white, they loom over you and shout in your face. They resort to disgusting behaviour and language, spitting obscenities your way. These outbursts, over a period of time, brainwash the victim into believing they are worthless. The victim in this scenario is baffled, lost for words, disabled and unable to respond. The victim is temporarily tongue-tied as the fear of the moment takes over and paralyses them. Their only thought is to calm the person down and get out of the situation as soon as possible. It is a dreadful feeling that you desperately hope never happens again. It always does! The controller has deliberately resorted to anger to get their own way and to ensure that they won't be challenged about any issues in the future. They will not be challenged. If you challenge this type of individual—do it at your peril! This is the lowest form of interaction between people. It is bullying and, it subjects another person to threats and possible violence, unless they do what they are told. It is cowardly. It stems from an inability to discuss calmly, fairly and frankly the issue in hand for fear of losing the argument or discussion and also losing control of another person or set of circumstances. The type of person that behaves in this way only loves themselves. They say they love you, of course they would say that, but do you really believe that someone who loves you would treat you in that way? On the other hand a controller who is in love is so afraid of losing that special person that they resort to unacceptable behaviour in order to frighten them into staying with them! This home is a household ruled by threats and fears. A household should be ruled by love and compassion.

Being on the receiving end of threatening behaviour is fearsome. Being confronted with bulging eyes and a tight-lipped snarl is scary and would make most people submit! In my opinion, a threat is a projected fear on the part of the person with the threatening behaviour. If the person exposed to the threatening behaviour can remember this during the time the anger explodes, then they might feel more able to deal with the outburst and react in a different way. The person threatening is the person who is scared and frightened and is projecting this fear onto their partner in the hope that the issue will go away.

They are becoming angry, safe in the knowledge, that their demonic persona will frighten the other person into total submission.

Examples
—When someone threatens to leave you if you do not comply with their demands
—When you feel forced to do something against your will
—When you are the subject of menacing behaviour
—When your every move is criticised
—When you are constantly watched
—When you are constantly ridiculed

Examples of Frightening Someone into Submission

In my opinion, women are the most likely candidates for this type of control! Women are easier to frighten into submission than men, I believe (there are exceptions, of course).

One patient I saw, on a fairly regular basis, could recount story after story of, in her words, 'having to submit to her husband's unreasonable behaviour and demands'. She didn't have to submit or respond to him—she knew that—she also knew the reason why she was giving in to him! She could not, and did not want to survive without him in her life! She believed that 'life would be unbearable without him'. She sabotaged herself. Her personality changed, her outlook on life changed, she put on weight, became unkempt in her appearance. She became anxious, depressed, and without hope for the future. She accepted life on his terms totally. She was afraid to make a decision on her own. He even tried to interfere with and tell her how to manage a very successful business she had built up, on her own, before she had even met him. Such was his need to control his wife! It was sad to watch this lady in her unhappy state. She knew that in order to be free again and live a carefree life she had to let him go, but she couldn't do it! Her doctor prescribed anti-depressants and, reluctantly, she accepted this in order to help her cope with living her chosen path. Her visits to me gave her the opportunity to unburden herself and tell an outsider of the quarrels and the situations that she was experiencing. Her husband gave her no emotional or physical support at home. She did everything to keep the house going, i.e. cooked for the family, cleaned the house, did the laundry for the family (always ensuring that he had a clean shirt and socks or 'war would be declared'). He, on the other hand, would come home from work, 'slob out' in front of the television, and that's where he would stay all evening. He would not budge an inch to get himself anything he might want, i.e., a drink, etc. The remote control would be at his side (or firmly gripped in his hand) and there he would be, in all his glory, controlling the entire household from his armchair! She felt foolish telling me of these scenarios and kept repeating, "I know I should leave him; you must think I am stupid and deserve what I am getting." She would also say, and believe, "Perhaps I've done something in my past and I deserve the treatment I am getting." Despite firm reassurances from me that I did not believe that this was so, she could not get these thoughts out of her mind. I urged her to continue coming to see me and, over a period of time, gently encouraged her to take back some control of her life by taking small steps to re-establish her self-respect. Her self-esteem had spiralled down so low that no amount of the 'talking therapies' would have worked alone. Shortly after being prescribed anti-depressants her energy levels began to rise and she was able to begin the journey of taking back some control of her life with regular counselling sessions.

Another story unfolded in a counselling session: A lady, who had been married for some twelve years, confided that there was a list of things that she could not do, at home, for fear of disapproval from her husband. These were:

—She cannot put nail varnish on her nails as he does not like the smell; it gives him a headache, and he becomes angry if she does this.
—She must not chew gum—he cannot stand the noise.
—She must not make conversation, whilst out socialising, unless he likes the person she is speaking to.
—He says she snores, or breathes too loudly, so he opts to sleep in the spare bedroom most nights!
—She must not fall asleep in the chair in the living room in the evening. If she does this he slams his hand down on the arm of the chair, or stamps his foot on the floor to awaken her (with a start!). He tells her that when she 'nods off' in the chair of an evening, she dribbles and looks ugly, fat, sexless and old!

—When they both go out for a meal and she chooses the table they sit at—he will always decide to sit somewhere elsewhere as her choice is unacceptable.

Negative Responses to Being Frightened into Submission
—Do as you are told at all times
—Never challenge your persecutor
—Jump, when asked to do something
—Dance to their tune
—Never share an idea or a thought
—Never voice your own opinion
—Accept that you are being totally controlled
—Accept your incapacity to change yourself and your situation
—Become anxious
—Become depressed
—Lead a stressful life

Positive Responses to Resist Submitting to Someone
—Don't respond/react
—Divert the conversation
—Challenge them
—Offer different options
—Realise they are cowards (knowing this helps to take some fear away)
—Stop being afraid of them and know they are afraid of reaching an outcome they can't deal with
—Stay in reality and in the moment—don't be tempted to imagine an outcome that affects your future with this person
—If he/she threatens to leave you—don't be gullible and believe him/her—ask yourself has he/she ever left you before?
—Stay focused on your inner state of mind and body
—Hold yourself still inside
—If you think the situation is going to spiral out of control and become violent—get the hell out!
—Smile, nod, agree and then do what you want to do

—Decide to change yourself

—Decide to change your responses

—Imagine you are someone else—how would they respond? If you discover appropriate reactions—try them!

—Disengage emotionally (this can be achieved with practice, as below)

—Imagine you are the third person in the room—stay with that person (in your mind) and observe both yourself and your partner. This exercise will help you disengage from the emotional entanglement you have become involved in.

—See you partner for who he/she really is—'knowledge is power'.

Step Four: To Control People, Situations and Outcomes

A controller always has to be the boss! They have to be admired and respected, and held in high esteem. They get this position by bullying and, usually, by holding the financial purse strings within a household. This person is obsessed with having their own way at all times. They believe that their thoughts, beliefs and actions are always right and should be adhered to by all the people within their rule. They are threatened by innovation, creativity and by someone who can 'hold their own' in social and professional situations. It is in the controller's interest to deliberately undermine any individual in their intimate circle who displays signs of being liked by others, getting ahead and becoming more successful than they are themselves. Controllers see themselves as supremely successful and liked by one and all. Really they are sad, failed individuals without any positive identity.

Examples of Control

A patient visited me because she was experiencing severe control issues with her husband. She gave me this example of a controlling feature she had encountered.

They were both going out to the pub one evening. Prior to leaving the house my patient had made some sandwiches and placed them in the fridge in the full knowledge that her husband would be hungry upon returning home from the pub. During the drive to the pub, my patient realised that her husband was angry but could not understand why! Of course, she asked him and he replied, "You should know why." She racked her brain and could only think of small, inconsequential reasons for his behaviour. Nothing significant had happened to provoke him to behave in a disgruntled, rude, obnoxious manner. When they arrived at the pub, they sat at the bar, as they usually did. He ordered his drink but ordered nothing for her! The owner/barman (who knew them both as regular customers) guessed that there had been a disagreement and gave my patient her usual gin and tonic. My patient's husband then turned his back on her and totally ignored her for the entire evening. The owner of the pub was especially kind and understanding (incidentally, he was gay and emotionally sensitive and aware), and fed her drinks throughout the evening, and behind her husband's back quietly resorted to calling him rotten for treating her in that fashion. When they returned home (the silence in the car was voluminous), she went to the fridge to give him the sandwiches she had prepared earlier. At this point she just wanted the evening to end. The children were in bed and she did not want to have a row that would wake and upset them. He didn't want the sandwiches and told her in a cold, threatening manner that he wanted scrambled eggs on toast. His words were, "Go to the kitchen and make me scrambled eggs on toast." So, the servile being that she had become, she went out to the kitchen and made the scrambled eggs on toast. On returning to the living room with them on a tray he looked at her in the most sinister way and told her he hadn't asked for scrambled eggs on toast, that he asked for poached eggs on toast. He said, "Go back to the kitchen and make me poached eggs on toast." She went back to the kitchen and made poached eggs on toast and brought them back into the living room on a tray only to be told in a frighteningly dark, demonic way that he hadn't asked for poached eggs on toast he asked for fried eggs on toast. Again he said, "Go to the kitchen and make me fried eggs on toast." So, she went back to the kitchen and was, by now, shaking in her shoes and scared stiff. She prayed that there were eggs left in the fridge! She wanted to grab the keys of the car and flee but couldn't because the children were upstairs in bed and she didn't want to leave them open to the possibility of being woken by her husband's ravings. There were eggs left in the fridge (thank God) and she made fried eggs on toast, and took them to the living room on a tray. When she presented this to him he said he had never asked for eggs in the first place—looked at her with complete disgust and contempt and went to bed.

She stayed downstairs for a long time and waited for him to drop off to sleep before venturing upstairs to the bedroom. In the morning, he behaved as if nothing had happened. He had exercised his masterful control; he had abused and bullied her to submission and was duly satisfied with the outcome. Of course he loved her!!!!!

Another example: Jill's father died. He had been diagnosed with cancer several years ago, but the ending came suddenly and unexpectedly. Jill was married and had three small children. When the death occurred, and after discussion with her husband John, she stayed at her mum's home, a few miles away, in order to be with her mum, accept visitors and to organise the funeral arrangements. Jill was away from her husband and children for four days. After the funeral, and later in the evening, Jill returned to her small family and began to relax for the first time since her dad had passed away. There had been no time for her to react to her dad's passing as she had been busy making arrangements and comforting her mum. When Jill and John went to bed that night, John wanted to make love to his wife but Jill felt unable to comply and confided in her husband that she had not had the time to come to terms with the death of her father and, having a vivid imagination, was worried that he might be standing at the bottom of the bed watching them having sex. John replied that that was okay because he had been meaning to tell Jill that he had been having an affair for the past couple of years and didn't need her for sex anyway!

Control and revenge at any price!

Negative Responses to Being Controlled
—Do as your told
—Never object to anything asked of you
—Be attentive at all time
—Put your needs at the bottom of the list
—Never expect anything
—Know your place
—Accept you are neither good enough or worthy to have an opinion or be listened to
—Be totally accountable to someone else
—Give in and give up on your wants, needs, desires.

How to Overcome Being Controlled in a Relationship
In my opinion, this will take a long time to overcome! In my book *My Way (How to Live Within a Difficult Relationship)*, I have devised a ten step guide to enable people to address this issue. I developed this strategy during the time that I was having problems within my relationship and have used this method with patients, during my career as a counsellor, with much success!

This is the outline of the strategy and ten step guide I developed in order to live within a difficult relationship:

—Step one—don't react
—Step two—be realistic
—Step three—stay focused
—Step four—devise a long-term strategy
—Step five—devise a short-term strategy
—Step six—make another small change in you (turn negative thoughts into positive thoughts—changing your thinking pattern)

—Step seven—observe
—Step eight—consolidate
—Step nine—review
—Step ten—continue the strategy

Step Five:
To Shift Blame from Yourself

The angry person is rarely wrong! You dare not offer them options or ideas to suggestions they makes If you do they usually reject them.

They are cunning and manipulative and get their own way by brow-beating their nearest and dearest. When suggestions are repeated to someone regularly, however bizarre the suggestions are, on a logical level, eventually you will begin to believe them! So, if you are told often enough that you are wrong and stupid, you will start to believe it and will stop making suggestions in the future for fear of looking stupid! When someone becomes angry they always blame the other person involved for pushing them to become angry! How many times have I heard patients tell me that their partner says "It's your fault I am like this!" or "You push me to the extreme and ask for all you get!" Another repeating pattern of an angry person is to deny that they have said something that clearly they did! Have you witnessed this conversation? "I didn't say that," you reply, "you did," and repeat in detail not only the conversation that took place, but where you both were, the time and date and what you were wearing at the time! Hot denial follows hot denial, eventually culminating in another outburst of anger. It is the angry person's way of stopping you in your tracks. They will not accept responsibility or accountability for their statements, actions or reactions, unless, of course, it suits them to do so.

Examples

A patient, who visited me, confided that they were even afraid to suggest a place to visit for a holiday. In the full knowledge that if the holiday destination was disappointing, they would be blamed and punished for the duration of their stay. They wouldn't give an opinion on what or where they would like to go on an evening out because they knew that if the evening turned out to be bad in any way they would be blamed. The same pattern would occur if they wanted to watch a television programme that turned out to be uninteresting to their partner. They would be blamed for making the wrong selection! They succumbed to agreeing with the partner's plans regarding any socialising, television programmes and future holidays—in order for peace to reign in the partnership.

The same patient told me that during an argument their partner (whom I am going to name John) would voice their opinions vociferously on a particular point and hammer the point home to them. My patient (whom I am going to name Janet) dared not argue with John at that time, so would just agree for 'peace at any price'. The following day, or, even, some hours later, when John had calmed down, he would completely deny that the conversation had taken place and that particular opinion had been voiced. John was either in total denial that he had made the statement, or felt foolish that he had caused such a severe argument to occur on an issue that was not only inconsequential, but total rubbish. John was always blameless and was cunning in shifting the blame of the argument to Janet. Janet's self-belief was low and, as a result of this, she was totally convinced that John was always right! This continued behaviour, on the part of John, led Janet into thinking and, temporarily, believing that she was losing her mind. Janet ended up not knowing if, when John said something, he actually meant it! Janet was totally confused.

A very tearful lady confided that she had felt forced to ask her daughter (sixteen years of age) to leave the family home due to an ultimatum issued by her husband! The sixteen-year-old had deliberately driven her mum's car, as a learner driver, and crashed it! The damage had been repaired and paid for by the young girl but the incident caused a furious reaction from her stepfather. There was no discussion—I am told there never was—just a statement from him, prior to him storming off in his car, saying "that girl had better not be here when I return!" My patient was frightened, scared, devastated; she didn't know what to do or where to turn! She eventually decided to confide in the mum of her daughter's best friend who, kindly, came to the rescue and offered to have the daughter live with them. When my patient's husband returned to the home, later that evening, he was very angry with his wife and *blamed her* for making the arrangements for the young girl to be re-housed elsewhere. He then proceeded to demand the return of the sixteen-year-old as soon as possible.

Negative Responses on How to Deal with Someone Who Shifts Blame
—Agree with them that you are to blame and accept it.
—Apologise, grovel, saying you are sorry repeatedly until you are forgiven.
—Enter into lengthy, reasonable explanations as to why you are not to blame (this is usually a waste of time as they don't listen)

Positive Responses on How to Deal with Someone Who Shifts Blame
—Stand up for yourself. (This needn't be done aggressively.)

—Continue to stand up for yourself on each occasion that arguments occur (again, do this non-aggressively). The saying 'gently, gently, catchy monkey' springs to mind.

—Decide on a course of action that you feel is fair and acceptable to both of you

—Remind yourself that you are dealing with a naughty child (there is a child in all of us and when the child misbehaves this knowledge, when brought to the forefront of your mind, will sometimes help with the way you react to situations)

—Reject the blame—emotionally—blame is a burden and is negative energy

—Know you are right (does it matter what they believe?)

—It is not your responsibility to explain, at length, every issue that is discussed—don't do this—as this response repeated, on a regular basis, will drain and deflate you. It also absolves the other person of responsibility and accountability

—Do not agree that you are to blame—not accept it emotionally—and carry on regardless

—Do not react to any verbal attack

—Divert the attack by introducing a different issue/topic (a temporary solution to an onslaught).

—Be as manipulative and cunning as them and, whilst acknowledging their opinion, not openly agree with them, but remove yourself from the situation and tell them that you need time to think things through.

Step Six: To Show Disrespect

To show disrespect is to show someone that you don't love or like them. It is the ultimate nail in the coffin of a healthy relationship. If a partnership has no mutual respect—there is no future! Respect is being civil and courteous and accepting that we are all different. Respect is being able to listen to what someone has to say without responding by ridiculing and hurting them. Treating others as you would want to be treated yourself!

Examples of Disrespect

Again, during a counselling session, I was told about a marriage that had separated. The husband and wife lived in separate towns but were attempting reconciliation. All seemed to be going well between them. He came and stayed with her regularly and gave every indication that the relationship between them was back on track.

One evening, just before they were to go out and meet friends in the local pub, the phone rang. She answered the phone—it was her house—and there was a woman on the other end of the line asking to speak to her husband. My patient was shocked, and handed the phone to her husband, saying that a woman was asking to speak to him. Her husband took the phone and spoke to the woman at length! After the conversation ended he told his wife that it was his right to speak to anyone he wanted to speak to whether it be at his wife's house or anywhere else. He had no conscience that he was disrespecting his wife's hospitality or that his wife had 'first call' on his loyalty, commitment and integrity. It eventually immerged that he had been seeing this 'other woman' behind his wife's back for quite some time and that this 'other woman' was pursuing him and quite prepared to break up a marriage, in order to 'get her man'.

Another patient told me how, if she displeased her husband, he would feel justified and pay her back, by turning his back on her, all evening, when in a pub having a drink.

This behaviour would continue until she grovelled and coaxed him back into a good humour.

To Show Disrespect Is
—Not giving your partner space
—Not acknowledging your input
—Not sharing your worries
—Not sharing responsibility and accountability for your joint lives together (financial, emotional, physical, spiritual)
—Deliberately hurting them
—Not catering to your needs whenever/wherever possible
—Undermining
—Intimidating
—Interrogating
—Not giving positive criticism
—Being inflexible
—Being uncompassionate
—Always expecting their own way
—By insulting someone and bullying them into surrender.
—Not allowing your partner a point of view and valuing their input
—By being cunning and sly in getting your own way.

Negative Responses in Dealing with Disrespect
—Accept being over-ruled
—Accept always that you are wrong in your thinking and responses
—Bow to the superior knowledge of your persecutor
—Accept you are unworthy, useless and incapable in all areas
—Accept you will not amount to anything
—Accept that you are nothing without your partner

Positive Responses on How to Deal with Disrespect
—Realise and understand that it comes from someone who does not respect themselves
—Stand up for yourself
—Make a stand and stick to it come hell or high water
—Love yourself—no matter what!
—Learn to respect yourself!
—Put your own needs first
—Value yourself!
—Appreciate who and what you are!
—Acknowledge your experience and wisdom and act on it!
—Don't react to unpleasant/inappropriate behaviour—just be still within!
—Realise that you don't have to react
—Remember that the little things don't matter
—Concern yourself with the bigger picture!
—Create a life for yourself (with or without your partner)
—Create your own security blanket! Give yourself rewards, treats.
—Learn to be self-sufficient!
—Tackle the obstacles that you have been scared of—trust me they will become easier!
—Learn to handle your own finances
—Be safe in the knowledge that the people you both come into contact with are aware of your circumstances and secretly support you.

Step Seven: To Criticise

The dictionary definition of a critic is: "One who expresses a reasoned opinion on any matter especially involving a judgement of its value, truth, righteousness, beauty or technique. One who engages, often professionally, in the analysis, evaluation or appreciation of works of art or performances. *One given to harsh or captious judgement*"(Merriam-Webster).

We are all critics! Criticism is an observation.

To be constantly criticised is to be constantly undermined. Criticism is a powerful tool, which, used consistently, will create a dependent, powerless, unconfident person who is unable to function alone. It takes away an individual's identity and ability to think or act alone. It is the start of a process of de-personalisation. The ultimate aim of criticism is to control!

Example of Criticism

A patient said that her husband apologised to people they were both in conversation with if, in his opinion, his wife said something that he did not agree with. This made her feel vulnerable and inadequate and resorted her to not taking part in conversations when he was present. He would make remarks, such as, "Don't mind my wife: she doesn't understand what we are talking about." In the early days of their relationship she confronted him regarding this only to be told that "it was a joke, and she was taking it too seriously". Some joke eh! At her expense! Making fun of someone else, in a derogatory way, is to criticise and undermine that person.

Examples
—Having the dishes examined after you have washed and dried them
—When doing the laundry Jane said that if one of the items fell to the ground, during the process of hanging the items on the washing line, her husband would be dissatisfied with the garment's cleanliness and would make her wash the item again.
—Being told you can't accomplish or reach a target as efficiently as your partner, from filling in crossword puzzles to furthering your career!
—Being told, repeatedly, that "you are nothing without me!"

Negative Criticism
Negative criticism is how we respond when we want to undermine another person in order to:

—Get our own way
—Feel superior
—Feel in control
—Apportion blame
—Make someone feel unconfident
—Make someone feel worthless
—Make someone feel unloved
—Make someone feel unwanted
—Make someone feel insecure

Positive Criticism
Positive criticism is how we respond when we want to help someone:

—To enable
—Offer logic

—To understand
—To assist
—To support
—To share
—To develop
—To evaluate
—To give confidence
—To make someone feel valued
—To make someone feel worthy
—To make someone feel secure
—To make someone feel loved

Negative Responses to Criticism
—Swallow it and allow the criticism to make you feel bad
—Feel vulnerable and weak
—Give up
—Say you will never do it again (whatever it is)
—Feel insecure and unloved
—Feel worthless
—Allow it to affect your life

Positive Responses to Negative Criticism
—Say thank you and ignore it
—Take it with a pinch of salt
—Realise who and where it's coming from, accept its source as clouded and unacceptable!
—Learn to detach from negative people who are controllers!
—Get constructive and valuable criticism from people you know love, respect and support you.

Step Eight: To Intimidate

This behaviour is activated in order to humiliate someone into submission (emotional or physical). It is always offensive, vindictive and cruel. It is a calculated way of controlling a person, persons and/or situations. It is an abuse of power and authority. Continued use of intimidation can wear an individual down to such a degree that they become dis-empowered and emotionally disabled. They become 'puppets' and can only do what they are told. This is mind manipulation/mind control. It is very powerful and the victim usually discovers that they have been the subject of this control too late to turn the situation around easily. The situation can, of course, be turned around. However, when you are afraid of your controller and you have been on the receiving end of years of intimidation, your energy, motivation, and belief in your own power is low and this is the reason it is difficult to turn the situation around to your way.

Examples of Intimidation
—Being shouted and/or sworn at
—Criticising
—Using threatening body language
—Being ignored
—Shifting blame to others
—Being told, repeatedly, that you are nothing on your own and that you need them as you are nothing without them!

—Never being allowed an opinion
—Everything you do or say is wrong

Example of intimidation: During a counselling session a lady told me that she was afraid to go to sleep at night because her husband said that he was going to kill her and the children when she slept. She felt that this threat had been substantiated when she had awoken one night to find him lying at her side, holding a mallet in his hand, which hovered dangerously over her head! His eyes were glassy and crazed, and, with his face right up to hers, told her not to sleep or he would carry out his threats. She told me that she knew, deep down, that he would not carry out the threat as he had never been physically violent in the relationship and he loved his children too much to ever do them any physical harm. Eventually she was to find out that this situation had arisen because her husband was jealous of her. She was a friendly, humorous, out-going and popular person with many friends and acquaintances. She was also devoted to her husband and her children and had never wanted to be with anyone else during the course of their marriage. She was unaware of his jealous nature and, therefore, could not understand his resulting behaviour. When she asked him what had she done wrong and why he was behaving in this way, he always replied menacingly, "You know what you have done." She didn't! The threats and intimidation continued and the fear it provoked in her resulted in this couple divorcing. When you are constantly intimidated to this extent, you believe and are fearful that anything is possible.

Negative Responses to Intimidation
—You can become indecisive
—Increase use of alcohol, cigs or drugs
—Less competent
—Under performing at work
—Vulnerable

—Inarticulate
—Stressed
—High blood pressure
—Isolated
—Sleeplessness
—Poor concentration
—Become anxious
—Become depressed

Positive Responses on How to Deal with Intimidation
—Realise what is happening and don't respond to the controller
—However tempted you are—don't react
—Change your response to the controller, i.e., before entering into any discussion with the controller, mentally run over the conversation that is going to take place and change the sequence and patterns of what you always say. If you do this, it will put pressure on the other person to change their responses.
—Put a protective barrier around yourself—you can do this through meditation
—Keep a journal of your repeated arguments and write down the reservoir of responses available to you
—Attempt various responses and reactions (as above) the next time the argument takes place
—Share your feelings with a trusted friend/member of the family for support
—Seek counselling (through your general practitioner/health centre)
—Decide to do something for yourself (a new hobby, a regular evening out, etc.) in order to raise your self-esteem and develop your confidence
—Learn a new skill (through you local college courses). This will enhance your self-image and offer you the opportunity of either becoming employed or getting a better job
—Acknowledge and value yourself and the skills and ability you already have

—Write out a mantra. This is a statement of what you want in, and from, your life! It need be no more than four lines. You can write anything you want, a good example might be: "I am as good as anyone else. I will improve, on a daily basis, to become emotionally and financially independent."

Step Nine: To Victimise

To victimise someone is to persecute them! To victimise someone is to 'pester' them!

Slow and deliberate pestering can wear an individual down into an anxious/depressive state of mind. Pestering (nagging) is to persistently annoy someone into surrender. "When persecuting/victimising someone you are subjecting them to harassment designed to injure, grieve and afflict"(Merriam-Webster).

Example of Being Victimised

The same lady I have referred to earlier (Step Eight—Intimidation) told me that she had tried, very hard, to mend her broken marriage with her husband. When they had separated she had moved out of the family home with her children and moved back to her mother's home nearby, the couple were in touch, daily, and he visited her mother's home every weekend to spend quality time with his children. The break-up was eventually accepted by both parties and they were both eager that the children would not suffer unduly by the split. During this time, on the weekend visits, they continued sleeping together and generally behaving as if they were still in a marriage. My patient was happy with this situation, as was her husband, as she wanted to reconcile with him and give the marriage a second chance. He gave her all the signs that this is what he wanted also. This situation was to continue for some eighteen months, and as time moved on, this lady slowly realised that she had become a victim, once again, of her husband's controlling behaviour. The weekend would begin with her welcoming him into her mum's home on a Friday evening with a hearty meal, wine and the warmth of a loving family atmosphere. The following day he would take the children on a day trip and she would never know whether she would be invited to tag along. She always was invited eventually, but the question always hung in the air until the last possible moment when he, grudgingly, agreed to her coming along usually after a request from one of the children. *Control!* It was dawning on her that even when they had lived together, permanently, her views had never been taken into consideration. Indeed she told me that when the family would embark on a day trip, she would not be allowed to suggest a place to visit. If she volunteered an opinion he would say quite curtly, "No one is interested in where you want to go; your opinion is unimportant." She also recalled being told, whilst taking their newly born baby for a walk in the pram, to keep her head down as she walked along the road, as she was offending passers-by because she was so ugly. *Victimising.* During the years she was married to him he had brainwashed her into believing that she was not up to much and "lucky to have met and married him". Slow and persistent victimisation had reduced her to believing she could make nothing of herself and her life and was, therefore, privileged and grateful to have him. Until, of course, the 'worm turned' and the couple finally divorced.

Negative Responses to Being Victimised
—Be at someone's mercy
—Smiling when you want to cry
—Pretending that everything is all right
—Tip-toeing around someone all the time (treading egg shells)
—Doing their bidding—no matter the consequences to yourself

—Give up on yourself
—Become non-descript
—Low self-esteem
—Blocking out your emotions
—Being unloved
—Flat-lining!

Positive Responses on How to Deal with Victimisation
—Take control
—Don't be afraid to show your feelings, learn when it is appropriate to do this
—Encourage open discussions, to enable you both to have a better understanding of each other
—Realise you are never going to get it right so stop trying
—Be reasonable, flexible and fair in your responses—but know when enough is enough (you will know when this happens by the feeling in your gut that screams—stop)
—Treat yourself kindly
—Realise how much you have achieved
—Don't be afraid to recognise your needs, wants and desires—you have a right to them
—Accept that you 'can't have it all' but make sure you 'get some'
—Take charge of you and know that any change you want to achieve in your life is up to you

Step Ten: To Bully

'Bullies are inferior, inadequate people.' They pick on sensitive, vulnerable people in order to feel superior. To bully someone is to abuse your power in the worst way possible. Slow, cunning and persistent bullying can make the most confident individual a 'gibbering wreck'. Bullies are predators, hunting to find their victims! Bullies never give up—hounding their victims until they completely surrender and have no self-worth or identity.

Example of bullying: A confident, articulate lady I once counselled was the victim of bullying. She told me that her friends were all surprised that she had become a victim to bullying from her husband! She was competent and able at holding down a responsible position of employment. Despite these circumstances, she succumbed to bullying. At first, of course, she didn't recognise that she was being bullied. She believed that all suggestions and advice were well meant and she listened intently when given any guidance and direction by her husband. She realised she was being bullied when she saw the reaction from her husband when she didn't take the advice/ suggestions offered! She was whittled down into carrying out his every demand in the fear that he would leave her. She loved her husband and wanted to be with him forever at whatever cost. The cost was high and she paid it! He ruled the roost! He called the tune and she danced it! The constant fear hanging over her head was that if she didn't do as he said he was going to walk out of her life forever. She couldn't cope with the possibility of living her life without the man she loved and be alone forever. This lady lived a double life. In the work arena she was a confident, able person who people turned to for help and advice. At home, she was a servile 'yes' woman who did as she was told. She did stand up for herself, on some occasions, but these were short-lived as the threatening reaction and outbursts of anger she experienced from her husband frightened her and quickly put her back into her 'rightful' place, beneath him! This lady tried all options available to her to change her husband. It took years for her to realise and accept that, with all the best will in the world, the only person you can change is yourself. She was scared to change herself for fear of finding out that he wouldn't love her if her behaviour changed and she became her own person. All she wanted was an equal relationship with him. Eventually, she had no option but to change some aspects of herself. She was becoming frustrated and grossly unhappy in the relationship and the choice became apparent that either she began the process of changing herself or ending the relationship she had fought so hard to keep. The process began and, thankfully, in the most part has proved successful!

The Negative Results of Bullying Are
—To experience being demoralised
—To be intimidated
—To be embarrassed
—To be humiliated
—To be ridiculed
—To be patronised
—To be criticised
—To be ignored
—To be dismissed
—To be over-ruled

Positive Responses on How to Deal with Bullying
—Don't respond
—Don't give up and give in
—Don't be afraid
—Stand up and be counted—a bully is a coward!
—Be brave and confront issues
—Realise the bully is a frightened, inadequate individual—not the threatening monster he/she appears to be!
—Be responsible for who you are and what you say
—Don't feel embarrassed when humiliated in public—other people recognise what's happening and the person is quickly identified as a 'bully' and disrespected and disliked
—Be strong and proud of who you are and what you have achieved
—Realise that you will be better off if he/she does leave you, there would be no more constant and persistent bullying to contend with
—If you feel that the bullying is going to turn into violence—*get out of the way and out of the relationship!*

Process of Change and Detachment

Detachment is not becoming emotionally involved in someone's control drama. It is a system of disengaging from a situation or person that is causing you to become distressed. Becoming embroiled in the control drama of another person weakens your mind and body. You become lethargic, vulnerable, pathetic, and unable to think for yourself. You are constantly fearful of the consequences of your speech and actions. When you experience these feelings, temporarily, you lose control of yourself. You are demoralised, depressed, anxious, helpless. You are a victim! You have given in and given up!

If you, actively, disengage emotionally from the argument, you will begin to strengthen your mind and, eventually, increase your energy. You can do this by taking a step back and slow the whole process down in your mind. Don't panic! Imagine a transparent, impregnable sheet of glass between you that stops hurtful remarks and accusations flying in your direction. By actively engaging in this simple task you will, automatically, distance yourself from the difficult situation you are in.

It is important to go through all the options that are available, and that I have outlined in this book, when dealing with a person who is angry on a regular basis. In order to accomplish this task, it is also important to protect yourself, emotionally, from possible, and probable, verbal attacks from your partner, etc. *(I am not talking about physical attacks as I firmly believe that if a relationship is physically violent you should end it!)* Protecting yourself will enable you to keep and build up your own energy. If, and when, for instance, you decide to change your responses during arguments your partner will not like the fact that you are not responding in your usual way and will do all they can to change the pattern of the argument back to the argument which always gives them the result they want.

During this time there will be a considerable amount of emotional tussling going on. Introduce any changes slowly and gradually. Too much too soon will only confuse your partner. You will need energy in order to stay alert, creative and spontaneous. Relax as much as you can, and reward yourself often. Recite your mantra at least four times a day and meditate on a regular basis. To become detached is to stay focused on yourself and the outcome you want to achieve. To disengage emotionally is not allowing yourself to be caught up in the time-wasting arguments that get you nowhere. When an argument begins:

—Be still in your mind and body
—Focus on your outcome
—Stay alert to what you want
—Introduce a response that is different from your usual response (but a safe one)
—Deflect the situation by agreeing, in some small way, to be part of the issue being discussed
—Don't raise your voice
—Quieten the situation down by not joining in and totally engaging in the argument.
—Allow the other person to rant and rave (to get it out of their system). Appear to be listening—but switch off—you have heard it all before—boring!!!!
—Don't get caught up, personally.

—Don't take any criticism personally
—Don't respond to intimidation (refer to the suggestions in this book regarding this)
—Don't respond to bullying (refer to the suggestions in this book regarding this)
—Don't show you are frightened. (Imagine your partner taking someone their own size with the same temper)
—Any personal insults coming your way—let them fly over your shoulder (it's always nonsense anyway).
—Imagine there is a transparent bubble around you. You can see and hear everything and they can see and hear you—but all harsh words bounce off the bubble and back to them. (This exercise works for me.)
—Try and end the argument by saying something like: "I need to go away and think about this—my head is full of thoughts that I can't put into words yet." This will give you time to decipher the argument (break it down bit by bit) and come up with a suitable, appropriate response that does not leave you feeling 'controlled and vulnerable'. You could share this with a close friend or counsellor who will offer you some options on how to respond.

I wish you the best of luck in dealing with the angry persecutor in your life. You can achieve a better quality of life. Don't despair. Keep on fighting. *You will get there!*

Life is transient—it depends on the mood of one
It doesn't depend on what you do—but the way in which
    it is done
Whether it be verbal, physical or mental
You have to choose your words
The pressure is on
The stakes are high
Your life is in a whirl
You fail in thought
You fail in speech
You also fail in deed
You can change the mood of one—so please yourself
    and be free
Free from torment
Free to breathe
Free to express your will
Begin anew with a fresh heart
The road ahead is peaceful and still!

Lightning Source UK Ltd.
Milton Keynes UK
UKOW050941241111

182618UK00001B/101/P

CARDIFF

AND BEYOND

CAERDYDD

A THU HWNT

Patricia & Charles Aithie

ALAN SUTTON

First published in the United Kingdom in 1994 by Alan Sutton Publishing, Phoenix Mill, Far Thrupp · Stroud · Gloucestershire

British Library Cataloguing in Publication Data applied for

ISBN 0-7509-0579-4

Welsh translation by W.J. Jones.

Typesetting and origination by Alan Sutton Publishing Limited. Printed in Great Britain by Bath Press Colourbooks, Glasgow

Cyhoeddwyd gyntaf yn y Deyrnas Gyfunol yn 1994 gan: Cyhoeddiadau Alan Sutton, Phoenix Mill · Far Thrupp · Stroud · Sir Gaerloyw

Gwnaed cais am Ddata Catalogio Llyfrgell Prydain mewn Cyhoeddiadau

ISBN 0-7509-0579-4

Addaswyd i'r Gymraeg gan W.J. Jones.

Teiposodwyd a chychwynnwyd gan Cyhoeddiadau Alan Sutton Cyfyngedig. Argraffwyd ym Mhrydain Fawr gan Bath Press Colourbooks, Glasgow

CARDIFF AND BEYOND

In 1801 the population of Cardiff was only 1,000, although it had a history that reached back beyond the Normans and the Romans to the Celts.

In the same way that oil has brought wealth to the most remote areas of the world, the small town of Cardiff rose to prominence through the excavation and export of coal during the Victorian and Edwardian periods. Cardiff became a City in 1905 by Royal Charter, and by the Second World War the population had risen dramatically to nearly a quarter of a million. Today nearly three hundred thousand people live and work here.

This collection of over ninety photographs of Cardiff and its surrounding area reveals the diverse and unique nature of this the capital of Wales. Stunning architecture with superb details, parklands, rivers and docklands are offset by images of the remote landscape and mining valleys that lie nearby.

CAERDYDD A THU HWNT

Dim ond mil o bobl oedd yn byw yng Nghaerdydd yn 1801 er bod gan y lle hanes sy'n mynd yn ôl tu hwnt i'r Normaniaid a'r Rhufeiniaid at y Celtiaid.

Fel y mae olew wedi dod â chyfoeth i rannau mwyaf pellennig y byd, tyfodd tref fechan Caerdydd i fod yn bwysig trwy gloddio am lo a'i allforio yn ystod oes Edward a Victoria. Yn 1905 daeth Caerdydd yn ddinas trwy Siarter Frenhinol ac erbyn yr Ail Ryfel Byd roedd y boblogaeth wedi tyfu'n ddramatig i ymron chwarter miliwn. Heddiw mae ymron dri chan mil o bobl yn byw ac yn gweithio yma.

Mae'r casgliad hwn o dros naw deg o ffotograffau o Gaerdydd a'r ardaloedd o gwmpas yn dangos y natur unigryw a'r amrywiaeth sydd ym mhrifddinas Cymru. Caiff pensaernïaeth drawiadol â manylion ysblennydd, parciau, afonydd a dociau eu hatredu gan ddelweddau o'r triwedd pell a'r cymoedd glofaol sydd wrth law.

ALEXANDER FOUNTAIN
FFYNNON ALEXANDER

Erected in 1860, the Alexander Fountain in Kingsway was named after the Mayor in 1859–60, William Alexander. It was sculpted by Wills Brothers of London and cast in iron by the Coalbrookdale Company. It was originally set into the St Mary Street Town Hall and depicts the story of Jesus meeting the Samaritan woman at a well (John, Chapter 4, verses 13–14).

Codwyd Ffynnon Alexander yn Rhodfa'r Brenin yn 1860 a chafodd ei henwi ar ôl y Maer yn 1859–60, William Alexander. Cafodd ei cherfio gan y Brodyr Wills o Lundain a'i chastio mewn haearn gan Gwmni Coalbrookdale. Yn wreiddiol, fe'i gosodwyd yn Neuadd y Dref yn Heol Eglwys Fair ac mae'n dangos stori Iesu'n cwrdd â'r wraig o Samaria ger ffynnon (Ioan, Pen 4, adn 13–14).

ALEXANDRA PARK
PARC ALEXANDRA

This ornamental park above Penarth Pier was opened on land donated by the Plymouth family in 1902 and named after the wife of King Edward VII. Apart from superb yew tree topiary and well laid out flower beds, the park also has one of the most beautiful war memorials, designed by Sir William Goscombe John RA, which was unveiled on 11 November 1924.

Cafodd y parc addurnol hwn uwch Pier Penarth ei agor yn 1902 ar dir a roddwyd gan y Teulu Plymouth ac fe'i henwyd ar ôl gwraig y Brenin Edward VII. Ar wahân i'r topiari coed yw ysblennydd a'r gwelyau blodau sydd wedi'u gosod yn rhagorol, mae gan y parc hefyd un o'r cofadeiladau mwyaf hardd a ddyluniwyd gan Syr William Goscombe John RA. Fe'i dadorchuddiwyd ar 11 Tachwedd 1924.

ARAB ROOM
YSTAFELL ARABAIDD

The interior decoration of Cardiff Castle is unique. Refurbished during the days of the coal boom, no expense was spared to create a visual celebration of nature, literature, philosophy and craftsmanship. The Arab Room in Cardiff Castle was built between 1880 and 1881, the year that the Marquess of Bute's architect and designer, William Burges, died. It is an interpretation of a medieval Middle Eastern room.

Mae addurniadau mewnol Castell Caerdydd yn unigryw. Wrth i'r lle gae ei ailgaboli yn ystod oes aur y glo, gwariwyd yn helaeth ar greu dathliadau gweledol o natur, llenyddiaeth, athroniaeth a chrefftwaith. Cafodd yr Ystafell Arabaidd yng Nghastell Caerdydd ei chodi rhwng 1880 ac 1881, blwyddyn marw pensaer a dylunydd Ardalydd Bute, William Burges. Mae'n ddehongliad o ystafell Ddwyrain Cano ganol oesol.

ATLANTIC WHARF
GLANFA IWERYDD

The opening of the orientally influenced design of the County Hall, by the former Prime Minister and Cardiff MP Lord Callaghan, was heralded by a spectacular firework display. Over half a million bricks went into its construction, and it now looms over the Bay.

Dathlwyd agor Neuadd y Sir, un a ddylanwadwyd gan yr orient, gan y cyn Brif Weinidog ac AS Caerdydd, Arglwydd Callaghan ar ôl arddangosfa dân gwyllt ysblennydd. Mae dros hanner miliwn o frics yn yr adeilad sydd erbyn hyn yn ymrithio uwch y bae.

BOER WAR MEMORIAL
COFADAIL RHYFEL Y BOERIAID

This bronze, between the City Hall and Law Courts, was designed by Alfred Toft, and is dedicated to the large number of Welshmen who lost their lives in the South African Boer War of 1899 to 1902. The sculpture depicts an Angel of Peace holding an uprooted rose bush. In its branches a bird is struggling to set itself free. It has been suggested that this is the most beautiful war memorial in Britain.

Fe ddyluniwyd y gwaith efydd hwn rhwng Neuadd y Ddinas a'r Llysoedd Barn gan Alfred Toft ac fe'i cyflwynwyd i'r nifer mawr o Gymry a gollodd eu bywydau yn y rhyfel yn erbyn y Boeriaid yn Ne Affrica rhwng 1899 ac 1902. Mae'r ddelw'n dangos Angel Heddwch yn dal llwyn rhosyn a ddiwreiddiwyd. Mae aderyn yn ei frigau'n ymdrechu i ymryddhau. Awgrymwyd mai hon yw'r gofadail harddaf ym Mhrydain.

BRECON BEACONS
BANNAU BRYCHEINIOG

Driving down the A470, to the west of Pen-y-fan, the highest mountain in South Wales, the smooth green flanks of Glyn Tarell reveal one of the classic views of the Beacons. This largely treeless landscape, created by underlying rocks of Old Red Sandstone, is ideal grazing land for sheep.

Wrth yrru i lawr yr A470, i'r gorllewin o Ben-y-fan, mynydd uchaf de Cymru, mae esgeiriau gwyrdd, llyfn Glyn Tarell yn dangos un o'r golygfeydd clasurol o'r Bannau. Cafodd y tirlun hwn sydd ymron yn noeth o goed ei ffurfio gan greigiau gwaelodol o Hen Dywodfaen Coch ac mae'n ddelfrydol fel tir pori i ddefaid.

BUTE STREET
STRYD BUTE

Bute Street developed as the
approach road to Pier Head during
the construction of the first dock in
1839, and the need to provide
housing for the influx of workers.
Much of the north end of the street
has been redeveloped; this southern
end, however, is the old business
quarter and still evokes the feeling of
its Victorian past. At night, in the
rain, it has an eerie quality.

Fe ddatblygodd Stryd Bute fel porth
i Ben-y-pier pan gafodd y doc cyntaf
ei godi yn 1839, a phan ddaeth
angen am dai i'r gweithwyr a
ddylifodd i'r dref. Mae llawer o ran
ogleddol y stryd wedi'i hailddatblygu;
ond yr hen ganolfan fusnes yw'r man
deheuol hwn ac mae'n dal i roi
teimlad o oes Victoria. Mae iddo
olwg iasol yn y glaw fin nos.

BUTETOWN
TREF BUTE

The view from the Marriott Hotel,
down Bute Street to the Pier Head
with its docks and cranes, is
unmistakable. It was here that thousands
of foreign sailors settled to make up the
community of Tiger Bay.

O Westy Marriott, mae'n amhosibl
camgymryd yr olygfa gyda'i dociau a'i
chraeniau i lawr Stryd Bute at Ben-y-
pier. Dyma lle yr ymsefydlodd miloedd
o forwyr tramor yn gymuned Tiger
Bay.

BWLCH Y CWM
BWLCH Y CWM

The forest around Castell Coch
creates a boundary between Cardiff
and the valleys. It is dense, and in the
autumn the deciduous trees form a
bank of vibrant colour up the hillside,
which rises to a favourite area for
forest walks.

Mae'r fforest drwchus o gwmpas
Castell Coch yn ffin rhwng Caerdydd
a'r cymoedd. Yn yr hydref mae'r
coed collddail ar lethr y bryn yn
ffurfio cefnen o liwiau byw sy'n codi
i fan poblogaidd rhodianna trwy'r
fforest.

CAERPHILLY CASTLE
CASTELL CAERFFILI

One of the largest and best-surviving
examples of a medieval castle in
Europe, Caerphilly Castle was built
in 1268 by the Norman baron and
Lord of Cardiff, Gilbert de Clare.
Besieged by the Prince of Wales,
Llywelyn ap Gruffudd, it was not
until 1271 that a hundred years of
building began once again.

Hwn yw un o'r cestyll canol oesol
mwyaf a mwyaf arhosol yn Ewrop.
Cafodd ei godi yn 1268 gan y barwn
Normanaidd ac Arglwydd Caerdydd,
Gilbert de Clare. Bu dan warchae gan
Dywysog Cymru, Llywelyn ap
Gruffudd ac roedd y flwyddyn 1271
wedi gwawrio cyn i gan mlynedd o
adeiladu ailgychwyn.

CANTREF RESERVOIR
CRONFA CANTREF

On the road to Brecon the Taff Fawr
is dammed in three places to form
the Cantref, Brecon and Llwyn-on
reservoirs. This series of reservoirs,
with their clay-earth cores, was built
originally by Cardiff City Council at
the end of the last century. Cantref
(c. 1892) is around 75 ft deep and
supplies water to the south-east
Wales grid.

Mae afon Taf Fawr yn cael ei
chronni mewn tri lle ar y ffordd i
Aberhonddu i ffurfio cronfeydd
Cantref, Aberhonddu a Llwyn-on.
Cafodd y gyfres hon o gronfeydd,
gyda'u craidd o bridd cleiog, eu codi
gan Gyngor Dinas Caerdydd ar
ddiwedd y ganrif ddiwethaf. Mae
Cantref (c. 1892) tua 75 troedfedd o
ddyfnder ac mae'n darparu dŵr i
grid De-ddwyrain Cymru.

CARDIFF BAY
BAE CAERDYDD

A major landmark of Cardiff
Docklands, the wooden signal
platforms of the inner harbour at the
Pierhead building once controlled
the arrival and departure of passenger
steamships. They were originally
connected to the quayside by a
floating platform and bridge.

Llwyfannau signal yr harbwr mewnol
wrth adeilad Pen-y-pier yw un o brif
dirnodau Dociau Caerdydd.
Unwaith roedd yn rheoli mynd a
dod agerlongau'r teithwyr. Ar un
adeg roedden nhw wedi'u cysylltu
wrth fin y cei gan lwyfan arnofol a
phont.

CARDIFF CASTLE
CASTELL CAERDYDD

A settlement has existed at Cardiff Castle for some two thousand years. Situated in the heart of the city centre, it has changed hands many times. The area was once occupied by the Romans and the Normans, and was in the possession of various families until it came into the hands of the Bute family in the eighteenth century. The 3rd Marquess of Bute appointed the architect William Burges to transform the castle.

Mae aneddfa wedi bod yng Nghastell Caerdydd am tua dwy fil o flynyddoedd. Mae wedi'i leoli yng nghraidd canol y ddinas ac wedi newid dwylo sawl gwaith. Fe fu'r fan yn eiddo i'r Rhufeiniaid a'r Normaniaid ar un adeg; wedyn bu'n eiddo i nifer o deuluoedd cyn dod i ddwylo'r Teulu Bute yn y ddeunawfed ganrif. Apwyntiodd 3ydd Ardalydd Bute y pensaer William Burges i weddnewid y castell.

CARDIFF CASTLE
CASTELL CAERDYDD

There are many spectacular elements to Cardiff Castle, but one of the most unusual is the roof garden. Designed like a courtyard with a central fountain, the walls are covered with hand-painted tiles depicting the story of Elijah and the prophets of Baal from the Old Testament.

Mae i Gastell Caerdydd nifer o elfennau trawiadol, ond un o'r rhai mwyaf anghyffredin yw'r ardd do. Mae wedi'i dylunio fel beili gyda ffynnon ganolog ac mae'r muriau dan orchudd o deiliau wedi'u peintio â llaw sy'n adrodd stori Elias a phroffwydi Baal o'r Hen Destament.

CARDIFF CASTLE
CASTELL CAERDYDD

As a central focus in the City of Cardiff, Cardiff Castle dominates the main thoroughfare. Although situated next to a busy commercial area, at the rear of the castle there begins a large expanse of parkland. The parks, exceptional in their beauty, are a credit to Cardiff, especially when so many European cities have lost theirs.

Ac yntau'n ganolbwynt canolog yn Ninas Caerdydd, mae Castell Caerdydd yn dominyddu dros y brif dramwyfa. Er ei fod wedi'i leoli'r drws nesaf i fan masnachu prysur, mae parciau eang yn cychwyn y tu ôl iddo. Mae'r parciau'n anghyffredin o hardd, ac yn glod i Gaerdydd, yn enwedig o gofio bod nifer o ddinasoedd eraill Ewrop wedi colli eu rhai nhw.

CARDIFF CASTLE
CASTELL CAERDYDD

The animals and birds on the animal wall outside the castle have been a source of enjoyment for all ages since the wall was built. They are attributed to Thomas Nicholls who did most of the carving at the castle. The wall originally extended to the front gate but has been moved, while some animals were added in the twenties.

Mae'r anifeiliaid a'r adar ar y mur anifeiliaid tu allan i'r castell wedi bod yn bleser i bawb ers iddi hi gael ei chodi. Thomas Nicholls a wnaeth y rhan fwyaf o'r gwaith cerfio yn y castell a dywedir mai ef a luniodd y creaduriaid. Ar un adeg roedd y mur yn mynd at y brif glwyd ond mae wedi cael ei symud. Ychwanegwyd rhai anifeiliaid yn y dauddegau.

CARDIFF CASTLE
CASTELL CAERDYDD

Little was known of pre-Norman Cardiff until the 3rd Marquess of Bute conducted some excavations at the castle. Workmen clearing a bank that had accumulated near the castle found an old Roman wall, part of which can be seen at the eastern end of the south frontage. It was duly preserved and a course of Red Radyr stone was laid to mark the boundary of the Roman wall.

Doedd neb yn gwybod llawer am Gaerdydd cyn y Normaniaid nes i 3ydd Ardalydd Bute arwain gwaith cloddio yn y castell. Wrth glirio bryn oedd wedi cronni ger y castell daeth y gweithwyr o hyd i hen wal Rufeinig. Mae modd gweld rhan ohoni ym mhen dwyreiniol ffryntiad y de. Cafodd ei chadw a gosodwyd cwrs o garreg Radur Coch i nodi ffin y wal Rufeinig.

CARDIFF DOCKS
DOCIAU CAERDYDD

The original docks were built in 1839 by the 2nd Marquess of Bute. Developed and enlarged, they are now operated by Associated British Ports with only a single point of access through the Queen Alexandra Dock lock. Coal, timber, grain, steel and oil still move through the port. Because the tidal range is so great it is possible to enter the dock lock only for around four hours before and after high tide.

Cafodd y dociau gwreiddiol eu hadeiladu a'u hehangu gan 2il Ardalydd Bute yn 1839 ond cânt eu gweithredu ar hyn o bryd gan Associated British Ports gydag un pwynt mynediad un unig trwy loc Doc y Frenhines Alexandra. Mae glo, coed, grawn, dur ac olew'n dal i symud drwy'r porthladd. Gan fod amrediad y llanw mor eang dim ond am tua phedair awr cyn neu ar ôl llanw uchel y mae'n bosibl mynd i mewn i loc y doc.

CARDIFF DOCKS
DOCIAU CAERDYDD

As part of the Severn Estuary, Cardiff Bay has one of the largest tidal ranges in the world. The movement of ships in and out is totally dependent on the tide. Only one ship is waiting here, but in the past many coal ships could be seen queuing up to enter.

Fel rhan o Foryd Hafren mae gan Fae Caerdydd un o'r amrediadau llanw mwyaf yn y byd. Mae symudiad llongau i mewn ac allan yn gwbl ddibynnol ar y llanw. Dim ond un llong sy'n aros fan hyn, ond yn y gorffennol roedd modd gweld nifer o longau glo'n ciwio i fynd i mewn.

CARDIFF DOCKS
DOCIAU CAERDYDD

Boston Buildings, in James Street, were constructed in 1900 by James Rose. In 1890, when the Clarence Bridge was built over the Taff, the area was a busy thoroughfare linking Butetown and Grangetown. The Boston Buildings originally housed a Danish firm, which might account for the mermaids.

Adeiladwyd Adeiladau Boston, Stryd James yn 1900 gan James Rose. Yn 1890, pan gafodd Pont Clarence ei chodi dros Afon Taf, roedd y fan yn dramwyfa brysur yn cysylltu Tref Bute a Grangetown. Roedd ffyrm o Ddenmarc yn Adeiladau Boston un tro a hyn efallai sy'n gyfrifol am y môr-forynion.

CARDIFF DOCKS
DOCIAU CAERDYDD

The detailed carving of a ship in full sail on the frontage of Baltic House in Mount Stuart Square is only one of many superb seafaring reliefs found in the bay area. This lovely six-storey building, dated 1915, was designed in an Edwardian Baroque style.

Dim ond un o'r cerfweddau ysblennydd o fywyd y môr a welir o gwmpas y bae yw'r cerfiad manwl hwn o long llawn hwyliau ar ffryntiad Tŷ Baltig yn Sgwâr Mount Stuart. Cafodd yr adeilad chwe llawr hardd hwn, sy'n dyddio o 1915, ei ddylunio mewn arddull faróc Edwardaidd.

CARDIFF MARKET
MARCHNAD
CAERDYDD

Regular markets have been held in Cardiff since at least the eleventh or twelfth century. The present Central Market was built in May 1891, although there had been an earlier covered market on the same site since 1835. The market was designed by William Harpur, the borough's engineer. It is basically a large wrought-iron shed, but is exquisite in its proportions and use of line.

Mae marchnadoedd cyson wedi cael eu cynnal yng Nghaerdydd er o leiaf yr unfed ganrif ar ddeg neu'r ddeuddegfed ganrif. Codwyd y Farchnad Ganolog bresennol ym Mai 1891, er i farchnad dan do fod ar yr un safle er 1835. Dyluniwyd y farchnad gan William Harpur, peiriannydd y fwrdeistref. Yn sylfaenol, sied enfawr o haearn gyr ydy hi, ond mae'r defnydd o gyfrannedd a llinellau'n rhagorol.

CASTELL COCH
CASTELL COCH

The original fortified red castle on the slopes of the Taff Valley was built by Gilbert de Clare, who was also responsible for Caerphilly Castle. Towards the end of the nineteenth century the Marquess of Bute commissioned the architect William Burges to rebuild it on its thirteenth-century ruins. By 1879 the design, building and structure of the rooms were finished. Although Burges died in 1881 with the bulk of the interior decoration still unfinished, it was completed in 1891 by craftsmen who had worked with him.

Codwyd y castell coch gwreiddiol oedd wedi'i gyfnerthu ar lethrau Dyffryn Taf gan Gilbert de Clare oedd hefyd yn gyfrifol am Gastell Caerffili. Tua diwedd y bedwaredd ganrif ar bymtheg, comisiynodd Ardalydd Bute y pensaer William Burges i'w ailadeiladu ar yr adfeilion o'r drydedd ganrif ar ddeg. Erbyn 1879, roedd y dyluniad, yr adeiladu a strwythur yr ystafelloedd wedi'u cwblhau. Er i Burges farw yn 1881, gyda'r rhan fwyaf o'r addurniadau mewnol heb eu gorffen, fe'u gorffennwyd yn 1891 gan grefftwyr oedd wedi gweithio gydag e.

CATHAYS CEMETERY
MYNWENT CATHAYS

Cathays Cemetery is the third largest
cemetery in Britain. Opened in
1859, many of Cardiff's founding
fathers are buried here together with
people from many denominations.
There is even an area of Chinese
gravestones. Today Cardiff City
Council is encouraging children to
learn from the cemetery through
heritage walks and nature trails.

Dim ond dwy fynwent ym Mhrydain
sy'n fwy na Mynwent Cathays. Fe'i
hagorwyd yn 1859 ac mae nifer o'r
tadau a sefydlodd Gaerdydd wedi'u
claddu yma, yn ogystal â phobl o sawl
enwad. Mae yma hyd yn oed fan sy'n
cynnwys cerrig beddau Chineaidd.
Heddiw, mae Cyngor Dinas
Caerdydd yn annog plant i ddysgu
gan y fynwent trwy deithiau
treftadaeth a natur.

CEFN ONN PARK
PARC CEFN ONN

One of the most outstanding parks in
Cardiff is Cefn Onn. Situated on the
northern slopes of the city, south of
Caerphilly, it comprises wooded
hillside and a dingle, which in spring
is a riot of flowering rhododendrons,
azaleas and new growth.

Cefn Onn yw un o barciau mwyaf
nodedig Caerdydd. Mae ar lethrau
gogleddol y ddinas, i'r de o Gaerffili
ac mae iddo ochrau bryn coediog a
llannerch sy'n fôr o flodau
rhododendron, *azaleas* a thyfiant
newydd yn y gwanwyn.

CHRIST IN MAJESTY
CRIST MEWN GOGONIANT

The magnificent aluminium sculpture of 'Christ in Majesty', by Jacob Epstein, is attached to a parabolic arch with an oval case, designed by the architect George Pace. It dominates the nave of Llandaff Cathedral, which was founded by St Teilo in the sixth century.

Mae'r gerfddelw alwminiwm ysblennydd o'r 'Crist mewn Gogoniant' gan Jacob Epstein wedi'i chysylltu wrth fwa parabolig a chanddo gas hirgrwn a ddyluniwyd gan y pensaer George Pace. Mae'n dominyddu corff Cadeirlan Llandaf a sefydlwyd gan Sant Teilo yn y chweched ganrif.

CHURCH STREET
STRYD YR EGLWYS

After the castle, St John's is the most interesting ancient monument in Cardiff still in use. The oldest surviving church in the city, dating from the twelfth century, it has had various restorations including its perpendicular pierced battlemented tower which is spectacular.

Ar ôl y castell, eglwys Sant Ioan yw'r cofadail mwyaf diddorol yng Nghaerdydd sy'n cael ei ddefnyddio o hyd. Hi yw eglwys hynaf y ddinas sy'n dal mewn bod, ac mae'n dyddio o'r ddeuddegfed ganrif. Mae wedi cael ei hadnewyddu nifer o weithiau, gan gynnwys ei thŵr perpendicwlar rhwyllog, bylchfuriog sy'n ddigon o ryfeddod.

CITY HALL
NEUADD Y DDINAS

Cardiff City Hall was one of the most outstanding municipal building achievements in Britain during the first half of this century. It is richly ornamented with expressions of various aspects of human endeavour: 'Unity and Patriotism', 'Science and Education', 'Commerce and Industry' and here, sculpted by Paul Montford, 'Poetry and Music'.

Neuadd y Ddinas Caerdydd oedd un o gampau adeiladu maestrefol amlycaf hanner cyntaf y ganrif hon. Mae wedi'i haddurno'n gyfoethog, gyda mynegiadau o nifer o agweddau ar ymdrech dyn: 'Undod a Gwladgarwch', 'Gwyddoniaeth ac Addysg', 'Masnach a Diwydiant', ac yma, wedi'i gerfio gan Paul Montford, 'Barddoniaeth a Cherddoriaeth'.

COOPERS FIELD
MEYSYDD COOPER

The large open parkland of Coopers Field next to the castle has always been a popular walk and recreation area for the people of Cardiff. In the early nineteenth century it was a favourite area on Sundays, when gymnastics and pitch and toss, a game where a coin is aimed at a target, were played.

Mae parc agored Meysydd Cooper gerllaw'r castell wedi bod erioed yn fan i bobl Caerdydd rodio ac ymlacio ynddo. Yn y bedwaredd ganrif ar bymtheg, roedd yn gyrchfan poblogaidd ar y Sul, pan fyddai gymnasteg a *pitch and toss*, gêm lle mae coin yn cael ei hanelu at darged, yn cael eu chwarae.

COWBRIDGE TOWN HALL
NEUADD Y DREF, Y BONT-FAEN

The history of the market town of
Cowbridge in the Vale of Glamorgan
stretches back to the Bronze Age.
There was a Roman settlement here,
and by the thirteenth century the
borough was considered second in
importance only to Cardiff. The
town hall on the High Street with its
attendant war memorial was
originally the county jail, until
purchased by the council in 1829
and rebuilt.

Mae hanes tref farchnad Y Bont-faen
ym Mro Morgannwg yn mynd yn ôl
i'r Oes Efydd. Fe fu sefydliad
Rhufeinig yma ac erbyn y drydedd
ganrif ar ddeg câi'r fwrdeistref ei
hystyried yn ail i Gaerdydd yn unig.
Yn wreiddiol, carchar oedd neuadd y
dref yn High Street, gyda'r gofadail
yn gydymaith iddi. Fe'i prynwyd a'i
hailadeiladu gan y cyngor yn 1829.

CUSTOM HOUSE STREET
STRYD Y TOLLDY

The Old Custom House (c.1845–65)
was built on the wharf of the Old
Glamorganshire Canal, with a dual
role of collecting customs duties and
as a seamen's shipping office. In its
day it was described as a 'plain
building inconveniently placed away
from the docks and an obstruction'.
Time changes attitudes. It recently
escaped demolition and has since
been listed and renovated.

Adeiladwyd Yr Hen Dolldy
(c. 1845–65) ar lanfa Hen Gamlas
Morgannwg. Roedd iddo ddwy
swydd, sef casglu tollau a gweithredu
fel swyddfa longau. Yn ei ddydd câi
ei ddisgrifio fel 'adeilad plaen wedi'i
osod yn anghyfleus ymhell o'r dociau
ac yn rhwystr'. Mae amser yn newid
barn. Cafodd ei achub rhag ei
ddymchwel yn ddiweddar ac wedi
hynny cafodd ei restru a'i
adnewyddu.

CYNON VALLEY
CWM CYNON

The current population of the Cynon Valley is around 63,000, yet when the first pits were sunk in the 1830s the area was a quiet farming community. The area near this street in Penrhiw-ceibr did not have pits until the 1850s, when families moved in and terraced mining cottages were soon built up. The chapel at the end of the street is a reminder of the importance of the Church in the valley communities.

Mae 63,000 o bobl yn byw yng Nghwm Cynon ar hyn o bryd. Eto, pan suddwyd y pyllau cyntaf yn yr 1830au, cymuned amaethyddol dawel a drigai yno. Doedd dim pyllau gan yr ardal hon ger Penrhiw-ceibr tan y 1850au, pan symudodd teuluoedd i mewn a phan godwyd nifer o dai teras y glowyr yn fuan. Mae'r capel ar ben y stryd yn ein hatgoffa o bwysigrwydd yr Eglwys yng nghymuned y cymoedd.

DRAGON
DRAIG

The 50-ft dome rising over the Cardiff Council Chamber is surmounted by a vast lead dragon, the symbol of Wales. It sits in a position of readiness for any attack. An unusually large-scale piece for the material used, it was cast in seven pieces by Messrs J.W. Singer and Sons from models by H.C. Fehr.

Mae gan y gromen 50 tr sy'n codi uwch Siambr Cyngor Caerdydd ddraig blwm anferth, symbol Cymru, uwch ei phen. Mae'n eistedd yn barod i daro. Mae'n ddarn anarferol o fawr o gofio am ei deunydd, ac fe'i bwriwyd mewn saith darn gan Messrs J.W. Singer a'i Feibion o fodelau gan H.C. Fehr.

Dyffryn Gardens
Gerddi'r Dyffryn

Dyffryn House and gardens have a history that goes back over a thousand years, when King Judhail gave the old manor to the Bishops of Llandaff before AD 640. The old manor has now gone but the moat that surrounded it still exists. In the sixteenth century the manor came into the hands of the Button family. A long succession of owners followed until it was rebuilt in the Victorian period and the gardens were developed. The present building, originally a stately mansion, has been transformed into a conference centre and hotel.

The 55 acres of gardens at Dyffryn House are full of colour and often described as gardens for all seasons. Around every corner some surprising shrub or sculptural figure surrounded by hedges is discovered.

Mae i Dŷ Dyffryn a'r gerddi hanes sy'n mynd yn ôl dros fil o flynyddoedd, i gyfnod cyn OC 640 pan roddodd y Brenin Judhail yr hen faenordy i Esgobion Llandaf. Mae hwnnw wedi mynd erbyn hyn ond mae'r ffos oedd o'i gwmpas yno o hyd. Yn yr unfed ganrif ar bymtheg daeth y maenordy i ddwylo'r Teulu Button. Bu mewn nifer o ddwylo gwahanol wedi hynny tan iddo gael ei ailadeiladu yn oes Victoria a phan ddatblygwyd y gerddi. Mae'r adeilad presennol, un a godwyd fel plasty urddasol, wedi'i drawsffurfio'n ganolfan gynadledda a gwesty.

Mae gerddi 55 erw'r Dyffryn yn llawn o liw a chânt eu galw'n aml yn erddi i bob tymor. Wrth droi pob cornel, rych chi'n dod ar draws prysgyn sy'n peri ichi ryfeddu neu lwyni o gwmpas cerfddelw.

ENTRANCE CHANNEL
SIANEL MYNEDIAD

This is the former entrance channel to the Roath Basin and Graving Docks. The intertidal mudflats of the Taff/Ely estuaries are feeding grounds for many thousands of wading birds during the winter months, notably dunlin, knot and redshank, which migrate to Scandinavia and Siberia for the summer breeding season.

Bu hwn unwaith yn sianel mynediad i Fasin y Rhath a Dociau Graving. Mae fflatiau llaid rhynglanw aberoedd Taf ac Elái'n feysydd bwydo i filoedd o adar rhydio ym misoedd y gaeaf, rhai fel llwyd y tywod, myniar y traeth a'r pibydd coesgoch sy'n hedfan i wledydd Llychlyn a Siberia yn ystod tymor magu'r haf.

EVAN JAMES AND JAMES
JAMES MEMORIAL,
YNYSANGHARAD PARK
COFADAIL EVAN JAMES
A JAMES JAMES, PARC
YNYSANGHARAD

This memorial in Pontypridd, designed by Sir William Goscombe John RA is to Evan James and his son James James, author and composer of the Welsh national anthem 'Hen Wlad fy Nhadau', who lived in nearby Mill Street. Ynysangharad Park is in fact a memorial park. Behind the monument, the war memorial on Pontypridd common can be seen.

Dyluniwyd y gofadail hon ym Mhontypridd gan Syr William Goscombe John RA i Evan James a'i fab James James, awdur a chyfansoddwr anthem genedlaethol Cymru, 'Hen Wlad fy Nhadau', oedd yn byw yn Stryd y Felin gerllaw. Mewn gwirionedd, mae Parc Ynysangharad yn barc cofadail. Mae modd gweld y gofadail ar gomin Pontypridd o fan tu ôl i'r gofadail hon.

FERNDALE
GLYNRHEDYN

Ferndale was once a quiet rural farming community, and even today sheep wander freely down its streets. When the first pits were sunk in the area the valleys changed beyond recognition, and the influx of allied trades and workers brought about the development of Cardiff and its surrounds. Terraced housing began to be built around the 1870s.

Cymuned dawel o ffermwyr oedd Glynrhedyn ar un adeg a hyd yn oed heddiw mae defaid yn crwydro i lawr ei strydoedd. Pan gafodd y pyllau cyntaf eu suddo yn yr ardal, newidiodd y cwm yn gyfangwbl ac wrth i grefftau cynghreiriol a gweithwyr ddod yno, datblygodd Caerdydd a'r ardaloedd o gwmpas. Dechreuwyd codi tai teras yn y 1870au.

FLAT HOLM
YNYS ECHNI

This small island situated in the Severn Estuary can be seen from many vantage points around Cardiff. Designated a Site of Special Scientific Interest in 1972, it is the home and breeding ground of many of the birds that fly above Cardiff's city centre.

Mae modd gweld yr ynys fechan hon sydd ym Moryd Hafren o nifer o fannau manteisiol o gwmpas Caerdydd. Cafodd ei dynodi yn Fan o Ddiddordeb Arbennig yn 1972 ac mae'n gartref a man magu i nifer o'r adar sy'n ehedeg dros ganol Caerdydd.

FLAT HOLM
YNYS ECHNI

Overlooking East Beach and the natural arch-like structure of Castle Rock near the landing stage for Flat Holm Island, one can just see Cardiff in the distance.

Wrth edrych dros y Traeth Dwyreiniol a strwythur naturiol tebyg-i-fwa Craig y Castell ger llwyfan glanio Ynys Echni, mae'n bosibl i rywun gael cipolwg ar Gaerdydd yn y pellter.

GARREG LWYD
GARREG LWYD

The remains of an Iron Age hut settlement lie on this sloping hill that overlooks the Rhondda Fawr above Blaenrhondda. The scattered rocks were believed to be sheep pens until earlier this century, when it was discovered that they were in fact dwellings of an ancient Welsh tribe, the Silures.

Mae olion caban anheddu o Oes yr Haearn yn gorwedd ar lethr y bryn sy'n edrych dros Rhondda Fawr uwch Blaenrhondda. Hyd yn ddiweddar, credai pobl mai llociau defaid oedd y cerrig gwasgarog, ond yn gynnar yn y ganrif hon fe welwyd mai anheddau hen lwyth y Silwriaid oedden nhw.

HAYES
YR AIS

The area of the Hayes is an ancient one. The name is derived from a Norman French or Middle English word meaning a hedge or enclosed space. From this elevated position above the compact area of the city, where once market gardeners delivered their goods using the canal that cut through here, one can see into the distance to the hills that lie between Cardiff and the valleys.

Mae ardal yr Ais yn hen. Daw'r enw o enw Ffrengig Normanaidd neu Saesneg Canol sy'n golygu perth neu fan caeëdig. O'r safle dyrchafedig hwn, man crynhoi'r ddinas lle roedd y garddwyr marchnad ar un adeg yn trosgludo'u cynnyrch gan ddefnyddio'r gamlas a dorrai trwy'r fan, mae'n bosibl i rywun weld i'r pellter at y bryniau sy'n ffin rhwng Caerdydd a'r cymoedd.

HAYES
YR AIS

This is overlooking David Morgan's, one of Cardiff's oldest department stores. David Morgan was a draper who began trading in the city when Cardiff was a major world port. At this level above the street Penarth Head can be seen, an illustration of how close the heart of Cardiff is to the sea.

Golygfa dros storfa adrannol David Morgan, un o siopau hynaf Caerdydd. Dilledydd oedd David Morgan a dechreuodd fasnachu yn y ddinas pan oedd Caerdydd yn un o borthladdoedd pwysicaf y byd. Ar y lefel hon uwch y stryd, mae modd gweld Copa Penarth, sy'n dangos i ni pa mor agos at y môr y mae Caerdydd.

HEATH ALLOTMENTS
RHANDIROEDD Y
MYNYDD BYCHAN

Better known as Flaxland Avenue
allotments, this is one of twenty-eight
sites in Cardiff covering some 190
acres with 3,000 plots. These
allotments produce a wide range of
vegetables and fruits including
potatoes, cabbage, outdoor tomatoes
and cucumbers, marrows, pumpkins,
sweetcorn, swedes, herbs, plums,
apples and damsons.

Mae'r man hwn yn fwy adnabyddus
fel rhandiroedd Flaxland Avenue ac
mae'n un o wyth ar hugain o
safleoedd yng Nghaerdydd sy'n
ymestyn dros tua 190 erw gyda 3,000
o randiroedd. Maen nhw'n
cynhyrchu amrediad eang o lysiau a
ffrwythau, gan gynnwys tatw,
bresych, tomatos awyr agored,
cucymerau, pwmpod, eirin, afalau ac
eirin duon.

HEATH WOODS
COETIR Y MYNYDD
BYCHAN

The area of Heath Park is now only a
small part of what was a large expanse
of common and waste ground that
extended from St John's parish to the
foot of Cefn Onn. The patch of
parkland that now remains has one of
the best examples of urban woodland
in South Wales. It was also the site of
a famous battle between the
Normans and Welsh princes.

Dim ond rhan fechan o'r hyn oedd
unwaith yn ehangder o dir comin a
diffeithdir yn ymestyn o blwyf Sant
Ioan at droed Cefn Onn yw'r ardal
hon ym Mharc y Mynydd Bychan.
Mae gan y clwt o dir parc sydd ar ôl
un o'r enghreifftiau gorau o
goedlannau maestrefol yn Ne Cymru.
Fe fu hefyd yn safle brwydr enwog
rhwng y Normaniaid a'r tywysogion
Cymreig.

JAMES HOWELL
JAMES HOWELL

This naturalistic detail decoration is on the frontage of the James Howell department store, which was built in 1879, fourteen years after Howell, the son of a Pembrokeshire farmer, set up a draper's shop in the city. Thirteen years later the expanded and renovated shop looked much as it does today. Built around the Old Bethany chapel it retained some of the original architectural features of the chapel in the interior. Howell also built the Park Hotel, and the Mansion House, once his private home, is now the residence of Cardiff's lord mayor.

Cafodd manylion yr addurnwaith naturiaethol ar ffryntiad siop adrannol James Howell eu llunio yn 1879, bedair blynedd ar deg ar ôl i Howell, mab i ffermwr o sir Benfro, sefydlu siop dilledydd yn y ddinas. Dair blynedd ar ddeg yn ddiweddarach, ar ôl iddi gael ei hymestyn a'i hailadeiladu, edrychai'r siop yn ddigon tebyg i'r hyn yw hi heddiw. Fe'i codwyd o gwmpas capel Bethany ac mae un rhan fewnol wedi cadw rhai o nodweddion pensaernïol y capel hwnnw. Cododd Howell hefyd Westy'r Parc, a'r Mansion House. Fe fu hwn unwaith yn gartref iddo ond arglwydd faer Caerdydd sy'n byw yno ar hyn o bryd.

KENFIG POOL
PWLL CYNFFIG

A short journey down the M4 towards Swansea will bring you to Kenfig Pool, the largest freshwater lake in the area. Part of a nature reserve, many wildfowl and birds breed here. The pool, dense with reeds, covers an area that was once a town. In the fourteenth and sixteenth centuries gales swept through the area engulfing the village with sand.

Ewch ar daith fer i lawr yr M4 tuag Abertawe ac fe ddeuwch at Bwll Cynffig, y llyn dŵr ffres mwyaf yn yr ardal. Mae'n rhan o warchodfa natur ac mae nifer o ddofednod gwyllt ac adar yn magu yno. Mae'r pwll yn llawn cyrs ac yn gorchuddio man a oedd unwaith yn dref. Yn y bedwaredd ganrif a'r ddeg a'r unfed ganrif ar bymtheg ysgubodd corwyntoedd drwy'r fan gan gladdu'r dref dan dywod.

LLANDAFF FIELDS
CAEAU LLANDAF

The large expanse of green fields at Llandaff is superb, and enhances the looming towers of the cathedral. In the autumn the richly coloured expanse of trees is the most notable feature. In the winter the great twisted branches are a highlight against the sky, creating one of the favourite avenues of trees in the city.

Mae ehangder mawr caeau gwyrdd Llandaf yn rhagorol ac maen nhw'n denu sylw at dyrau ymrithiol y gadeirlan. Yn yr hydref, yr ehangder cyfoethog o goed yw ei brif nodwedd. Pan ddaw'r gaeaf, mae'r cangau mawr cordeddog yn amlwg yn erbyn yr awyr ac yn creu un o rodfeydd coed mwyaf dewisol y ddinas.

LLANISHEN RESERVOIR
CRONFA DDŴR
LLANISIEN

Built by Cardiff City Council in 1886 with an earth embankment and clay core, Llanishen Reservoir was transferred to Welsh Water in the 1970s. Together with the Lisvane Reservoir it is used principally for recreation, trout fishing and sailing, and not for supplying water.

Cafodd ei chodi gan Gyngor Dinas Caerdydd yn 1886. Mae iddi wrthglawdd o bridd a chraidd o glai. Fe'i trosglwyddwyd i Dŵr Cymru yn y 1970au. Ynghyd â chronfa ddŵr Llys-faen, caiff ei defnyddio'n bennaf ar gyfer adloniant, pysgota brithyllod a hwylio ac nid i gyflenwi dŵr.

LLANTWIT MAJOR
LLANILLTUD FAWR

One of the most interesting places in the Vale beyond Cardiff is Llantwit Major. It has an ancient local Welsh history; later the Romans settled here and perhaps a Christian church (some suggest the first in Wales) was built here. The beach is one of the wonders of the coastline with its flat Lias Limestone platforms. The sea dashes in at tremendous speed against the cliffs and throws up large rounded boulders, which roll across the beach. It is not unusual during a storm for the light to break through the clouds to illuminate the whole beach.

Llanilltud Fawr, tu draw i Gaerdydd, yw un o'r mannau mwyaf diddorol ym Mro Morannwg. Mae i'r fan hanes lleol Cymreig hynafol; yn ddiweddarach sefydlodd y Rhufeiniaid yma ac efallai eglwys Gristnogol (y gyntaf yng Nghymru, yn ôl rhai). Mae'r traeth yn un o ryfeddodau'r arfordir gyda'i lwyfan gwastad o Galchfaen Lias. Fe hyrddia'r tonnau'n chwim yn erbyn y clogwyni gan daflu i fyny feini mawrion crwn sy'n rowlio ar draws y traeth. Dyw hi ddim yn anghyffredin yn ystod storm i olau dorri trwy'r cymylau gan oleuo'r holl draeth.

MAESYFELIN
MAESYFELIN

This neolithic chambered tomb at St Lythans consists of three mudstone slabs and a capstone. Human remains and pottery have been found here, suggesting that it is a ritual burial ground. Its maximum internal height is about 5 ft.

Mae'r bedd siambr neolithig hwn yn Llwyneliddon yn cynnwys tri slab carreg laid a maen capan. Maen nhw wedi dod o hyd i olion dynol a chrochenwaith yma, sy'n awgrymu mai tir claddu defodol oedd yma. Yn ei fan mewnol uchaf mae tua 5 tr.

MORGAN ARCADE
ARCÊD MORGAN

Often described as the City of Arcades, Cardiff has been lucky to have retained much of the character and original features of its Victorian arcades. Morgan Arcade, built over a period of three years between 1896 and 1899, is attached to David Morgan's, and is a perfect example of a covered shopping area.

Caiff Caerdydd ei disgrifio'n aml fel Dinas yr Arcedau ac mae wedi bod yn lwcus i gael cadw llawer o gymeriad a nodweddion gwreiddiol ei harcedau Victoraidd. Cafodd Arcêd Morgan ei hadeiladu dros gyfnod o dair blynedd, rhwng 1896 ac 1899. Mae wedi'i chysylltu wrth siop David Morgan ac mae'n enghraifft berffaith o ardal siopa dan do.

NATIONAL MUSEUM
AMGUEDDFA
GENEDLAETHOL

The foundation stone for the National Musuem was laid by King George V in 1912 but, due to the First World War, completion was delayed and the museum was not opened until 1927. Its eastern wing with the Rheardon-Smith Lecture Theatre was finished in 1932. New galleries were opened by Queen Elizabeth II in October 1993.

Gosodwyd carreg sylfaen yr Amgueddfa Genedlaethol gan y Brenin Siôr V yn 1912, ond oherwydd y Rhyfel Byd Cyntaf bu oedi cyn cwblhau'r adeilad ac ni chafodd ei agor tan 1927. Cafodd yr aden ddwyreiniol, gyda Theatr Ddarlithio Reardon Smith, ei chwblhau yn 1932. Agorwyd orielau newydd gan y Frenhines Elizabeth yn Hydref 1993.

NATIONAL MUSEUM
AMGUEDDFA
GENEDLAETHOL

The museum has many interesting and unique exhibits, including many that reflect various aspects of Welsh heritage and an internationally renowned collection of Impressionist art, bequeathed to the museum by coal heiresses Margaret and Gwendoline Davies.

Mae gan yr amgueddfa nifer o arddangosiadau diddorol ac unigryw, gan gynnwys rhai sy'n adlewyrchu agweddau gwahanol ar y dreftadaeth Gymreig. Caiff ei chydnabod yn rhyngwladol am ei chasgliad enwog o gelfyddyd Argraffiadol a roddwyd iddi gan yr etifeddesau glo, Margaret a Gwendoline Davies.

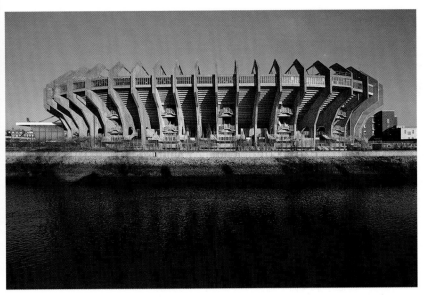

NATIONAL STADIUM
STADIWM GENEDLAETHOL

Otherwise known as Cardiff Arms Park, the National Stadium has a long history. It started on a piece of ground that was believed to have been the site of the ancient town green. Cardiff Football Club, later Cardiff RFC, was founded here in 1876. The first International game was held in 1884.

Enw arall ar hon yw Parc yr Arfau, ac mae iddi hanes hir. Cychwynnodd ar ddarn o dir a oedd, yn ôl un gred, yn rhan o lain werdd y dref. Sefydlwyd Clwb Pêl-droed Caerdydd, yn ddiweddarach CR Caerdydd, yn 1876. Fe fu'r gêm ryngwladol gyntaf yma yn 1884.

NAVIGATION STATUE
CERFDDELW FORDWYOL

The navigation statue by Albert Hodge flanks the entrance steps to the old Glamorgan County Hall in Cathays Park. Dating from 1912, it won a major architectural prize in its day. It is now used by the present Mid-Glamorgan County Council. The sculptures, with their impression of powerful swift movement, symbolize the canal transportation that brought the coal down from the valleys to Cardiff.

Mae'r gerfddelw fordwyol gan Albert Hodge wrth ystlys grisiau'r porth i Hen Neuadd Sir Morgannwg ym Mharc Cathays. Mae'n dyddio o 1912 ac enillodd brif wobr bensaernïol yn ei dydd. Caiff ei defnyddio ar hyn o bryd gan y Cyngor Sir Morgannwg Ganol presennol. Mae'r delwau, sy'n rhoi'r argraff o symud nerthol a chwim, yn symboleiddio trafnidiaeth y gamlas a ddeuai â glo i lawr o'r cymoedd i Gaerdydd.

NORWEGIAN CHURCH
EGLWYS NORWYAIDD

Built in 1868, the Norwegian church in Cardiff Bay was the first Norwegian seamen's mission to be built abroad. Founded for the Scandinavian sailors who brought pit props to the South Wales valleys and staffed British Merchant Navy ships, it was dismantled and saved by the Norwegian Church Preservation Trust in the 1980s.

Codwyd yr Eglwys Norwyaidd ym Mae Caerdydd yn 1868. Hi yw'r eglwys genhadol Norwyaidd gyntaf i gael ei hadeiladu dros y môr. Fe'i sefydlwyd ar gyfer y morwyr o Lychlyn a ddeuai â phropiau pyllau i gymoedd De Cymru ac a weithiai ar Longau Masnach Llynges Prydain. Fe'i datgymalwyd a'i hachub gan Ymddiriedolaeth Cadw'r Eglwys Norwyaidd yn y 1980au.

PEACOCK
PAUN

There have been peacocks in Cardiff Castle grounds since the nineteenth century. These were probably imported from India or south-east Asia where they are native. The present muster, which stay out of doors all year, were introduced in 1968. They roost in the Castle's tall trees at night and the hens lay clutches of eggs not in a nest but in a scrape in the ground among the bushes.

Mae peunod wedi bod at diroedd Castell Caerdydd er y bedwaredd ganrif ar bymtheg. Mae'n bosib iddyn nhw gael eu mewnforio o India neu Dde-ddwyrain Asia, eu cynefin. Cafodd yr haid bresennol, sy'n byw yn yr awyr agored drwy'r flwyddyn, eu cyflwyno yn 1968. Maen nhw'n clwydo yng ngoed tal y Castell wedi iddi nosi. Dyw'r ieir ddim yn dodwy eu hwyau mewn nythod ond ar grafiad o dir yng nghanol y llwyni.

PENARTH
PENARTH

The view from the park at the end of Penarth Head Lane is exceptional. From here it is possible to see all the way to Lavernock Point, to which Guglielmo Marconi successfully transmitted the world's first wireless message across the sea from Flat Holm island in 1897.

Mae'r olygfa o ben draw Lôn Copa Penarth o'r parc yn eithriadol. O'r fan hon mae'n bosibl gweld yr holl ffordd i Drwyn Larnog lle y bu Marconi'n trawsyrru negesau radio'n llwyddiannus ar draws y môr o Ynys Echni yn 1897.

PENARTH PIER
PIER PENARTH

The 600 ft long pier in Penarth was built in 1894. It caught fire in 1931 and in 1947 was hit by a Canadian steamer. Renovations have helped it to survive the ravages of time, and the last one gave it a wonderful Art Deco pavilion.

Codwyd pier Penarth, sy'n 600 tr o hyd, yn 1894. Aeth ar dân yn 1931 ac yn 1947 cafodd ei daro gan stemar o Ganada. Mae adnewyddiadau wedi ei helpu i wrthsefyll traul amser, a chafodd bafiliwn Celfyddyd Deco rhyfeddol gan yr un olaf.

PENARTH PORTWAY MARINA
MARINA FFORDD BORTHLADD PENARTH

Penarth Docks were opened in 186
for the loading of steam coal, and a
their peak in 1916 they handled 3½
million tons of coal. Since they wer
closed to shipping in 1963 a new
development of housing has been
established near the Old Customs
House and marine buildings, which
are all listed for special architectural
and historic interest.

Agorwyd Dociau Penarth yn 1865
gyfer llwytho glo rhydd. Pan oedde
nhw ar eu gorau yn 1916 roedden
nhw'n trin 3½ miliwn o dunelli o lo
Ers iddyn nhw gael eu cau i longau
yn 1963 mae tai newydd wedi cael
eu hadeiladu ger yr Hen Dolldy a'r
adeiladau morol. Maen nhw i gyd
wedi'u rhestru oherwydd eu
diddordeb pensaernïol a hanesyddo
arbennig.

PETERSTONE–SUPER–E
LLANBEDR–Y–FRO

Although Peterstone-Super-Ely is
only a stone's throw from the busy
centre of Cardiff, it would be easy
think you were in the heart of Wal
The area is a reminder of how rare
is to find so much countryside arou
a European capital city. This sheep
dog owned by a local farmer spent
half an hour jumping through the
farm gate.

Er nad yw Llanbedr-y-fro ond tafli
carreg o ganolfan brysur Caerdydd
byddai'n hawdd ichi gredu eich bo
yng nghanol Cymru. Mae'r ardal y
eich atgoffa o pa mor anghyffredin
hi i ddod o hyd i gymaint o gefn
gwlad o gwmpas prifddinas
Ewropeaidd. Treuliodd y ci defaid
hwn sy'n eiddo i ffermwr lleol han
awr yn neidio trwy glwyd y fferm.

PIERHEAD BUILDING
ADEILAD PEN Y PIER

The Pierhead Building was originally
built for the Cardiff Railway
Company in 1896 by the architect
William Frame, an assistant to
William Burges who renovated
Cardiff Castle. Listed Grade I, it is an
exceptional building of its period,
and of immense historical value to
the docks. Its style portrays many
influences from countries of the
former Empire, particularly of the red
Moghul buildings of India.

Cafodd yr adeilad Pen y pier hwn ei
godi'n wreiddiol yn 1896 gan y
pensaer William Frame ar gyfer
Cwmni Rheilffordd Caerdydd.
Roedd ef yn gynorthwydd i William
Burges a adnewyddodd Gastell
Caerdydd. Mae wedi'i restru'n Radd
1 ac mae'n adeilad eithriadol o'i
gyfnod ac o werth hanesyddol
amhrisiadwy i'r dociau. Mae ei
arddull yn portreadu nifer o
ddylanwadau o wledydd y
Gymanwlad gynt, yn enwedig
adeiladau Moghul coch India.

PIERHEAD BUILDING
ADEILAD PEN Y PIER

A terracotta detail from one of the
many on the exterior of the Pierhead
building.

Un o'r nifer o fanylion teracota ar
allanolion adeilad pen y pier.

PONTYPRIDD BRIDGE
PONT PONTYPRIDD

Built in 1756, Pontypridd's old bridge over the River Taff was probably the largest single-span bridge in Europe. At 140 ft it was an engineering feat, and was designed by a local minister, the Revd William Edwards. Today it is still used by pedestrians although it has a very steep camber.

Codwyd hen bont Pontypridd dros Afon Taf yn 1756 ac mae'n bosibl mai hi oedd y bont un rhychwant fwyaf yn Ewrop ar un adeg. Mae'n 140 tr ac yn gamp beirianyddol. Cafodd ei dylunio gan weinidog lleol, y Parchg. William Edwards. Mae teithwyr ar droed yn dal i'w defnyddio er bod iddi grymder serth iawn.

PONTCANNA FIELDS
CAEAU PONTCANNA

No other capital city in Europe has so much parkland in its centre as does Cardiff. Pontcanna Fields on the west side of the River Taff is part of the superb green area of the city. On this day the frost had taken hold, giving the park a chilly beauty.

Does gan yr un brifddinas arall yn Ewrop gymaint â Chaerdydd o dir glas yn ei chanol. Mae Caeau Pontcanna, ar ochr orllewinol Afon Taf, yn rhan o ardal werdd odidog y ddinas. Ar y diwrnod hwn, roedd y rhew wedi gafael, gan beri i'r parc fod yn iasol o hardd.

PONTYPRIDD COMMON
COMIN PONTYPRIDD

There are two old stone circles on Pontypridd Common. This one was erected in 1860 by Evan Davies, or Myfyr Morgannwg, who was involved in the local druidic practices of the nineteenth century. It is a symbolic representation of a serpent.

Ceir dau hen gylch ar Gomin Pontypridd. Codwyd yr un yma yn 1860 gan Evan Davies, neu Myfyr Morgannwg, a oedd yn cymryd rhan mewn arferion derwyddôl lleol yn y bedwaredd ganrif ar bymtheg. Mae'n symboleiddio sarff.

PORTHKERRY BEACH
TRAETH PORTHCERI

West of Cardiff lies Porthkerry Beach. Its importance goes back to Roman times when there was a lighthouse here. Today the steep bank of pebbles leading down to the sea is a favourite place for people to sit and watch the ships moving up and down the Bristol Channel.

Mae Traeth Porthceri i'r gorllewin o Gaerdydd ac aiff ei bwysigrwydd yn ôl i adeg y Rhufeiniaid pan oedd goleudy yma. Heddiw mae'r llethr serth o gerigos sy'n arwain i lawr i'r môr yn fan poblogaidd i bobl eistedd arno i wylio'r llongau'n hwylio i fyny ac i lawr Môr Hafren.

QUEEN ALEXANDRA DOCK
DOC Y FRENHINES ALEXANDRA

The Queen Alexandra Dock is the largest and most modern dock in Cardiff. Built between 1897 and 1907 it covers an area of 52 acres, but unlike many other docks in the complex is still in use. Along with the nearby Roath Dock, it is one of the largest walled docks in existence. When it was opened by King Edward VII and Queen Alexandra in 1907, Cardiff was one of the busiest ports in the world.

Doc y Frenhines Alexandra yw doc mwyaf a mwyaf modern Caerdydd. Cafodd ei adeiladu rhwng 1897 a 1907 ac mae'n ymestyn dros 52 o erwau; ond yn wahanol i sawl doc arall caiff y cymhlygion eu defnyddio o hyd. Ynghyd â Doc y Rhath cyfagos, ef yw un o'r dociau muriog mwyaf sy'n bod. Pan gafodd ei agor gan y Brenin Edward VII a'r Frenhines Alexandra yn 1907, Caerdydd oedd un o borthladdoedd prysuraf y byd.

RHONDDA VALLEY
CWM RHONDDA

This view looks down upon Hopkinstown and Porth where the River Rhondda flows south towards the Taff. With the decline of the coal industry, the scarred hillsides are gradually being reclaimed by nature.

Mae'r olwg hon yn edrych i lawr ar Drehopcyn a'r Porth lle mae Afon Rhondda'n llifo i'r de tuag Afon Taf. Gyda machlud y diwydiant glo, mae natur yn adennil yr esgeiriau creithiog yn raddol.

RHONDDA VALLEY
CWM RHONDDA

The towering hills overlooking Cwm-parc, an old colliery village adjacent to Treorchy in Rhondda Fawr, have some of the most superb views in Glamorgan. The car park at Bwlch y Clawdd, however, is not such a quiet place to contemplate. It is home to a flock of sheep that has developed a voracious appetite for ice-cream and hamburger buns.

O'r bryniau tyrog sy'n edrych dros Gwm-parc, hen bentref glofaol gerllaw Treorci yn Rhondda Fawr, fe gewch un o'r golygfeydd mwyaf ysblennydd ym Morgannwg. Fodd bynnag, go brin fod maes parcio Bwlch y Clawdd yn lle mor dawel â hynny i fyfyrio ynddo. Mae'n gartref i braidd o ddefaid sy wedi magu archwaeth wancus at hufen iâ a byniau hamnionod.

ROATH PARK
PARC Y RHATH

The autumn ground detail in any large park often suggests more about the variety of plants and trees than any ordinary picture can do.

Yn aml, mae golwg fanwl ar dir yr hydref mewn sawl parc mawr yn awgrymu mwy am yr amrywiaeth o blanhigion a choed nag a wna unrhyw ddarlun cyffredin.

ROATH PARK
PARC Y RHATH

The Scott Memorial Lighthouse at Roath Park was built as a memorial to Captain Scott's expedition to the Antarctic. The journey was supported by sponsorship raised by the people of Cardiff. The *Terra Nova*, which left from the city's Bute Docks in 1910, is represented on the weathervane at the top of the monument.

Fe godwyd Goleudy Coffa Scott ym Mharc y Rhath i gofio am alldaith Capten Scott i'r Antarctig. Cafodd y daith ei chefnogi gan nawdd a godwyd gan bobl Caerdydd. Caiff y *Terra Nova*, a hwyliodd o Ddociau Bute yn 1910, ei chynrychioli ar y ceiliog gwynt ar frig y gofadail.

ST DAVID'S HALL
NEUADD DEWI SANT

When the Revd Eli Jenkins declared 'Thank God we are a musical nation', in Dylan Thomas's *Under Milk Wood*, he was not joking. The concert hall is now a venue for many international concerts, competitions and entertainment, and famous for its use of white concrete in the interior.

Pan ddatganodd y Parchedig Eli Jenkins, 'Thank God we are a musical nation', yn *Under Milk Wood* gan Dylan Thomas, doedd e ddim yn cellwair. Mae'r neuadd gyngerdd yn awr yn gyrchfan i nifer o gyngherddau rhyngwladol, cystadlaethau ac adloniant ac mae'n enwog am y defnydd o goncrit gwyn tu mewn.

St David's Hall
Neuadd Dewi Sant

This detail of the stained glass window in St David's Hall is only a small part of a gigantic panel of painted glass by the German artist Hans Gottfried von Stockhausen, which was presented to Cardiff by the people of its twin city of Stuttgart in 1985. Using the visual elements of a large deep-rooted tree set in a landscape, it is symbolic of the spirit of Wales and its historical and cultural significance.

Dyw'r manylyn hwn o'r gwydr lliw yn Neuadd Dewi Sant yn ddim ond rhan fechan o banel anferth o wydr lliw gan yr arlunydd o'r Almaen, Hans Gottfried von Stockhausen, a gafodd ei gyflwyno i Gaerdydd gan bobl Stuttgart, ei hefeilldref, yn 1985. Gan ddefnyddio elfennau gweledol o goeden fawr, dwfn ei gwreiddiau, wedi'i gosod mewn tirlun, mae'n symbol o ysbryd Cymru a'i arwyddocâd hanesyddol a diwylliannol.

St Fagans
Sain Ffagan

One of the many buildings brought to the Welsh Folk Museum at St Fagans as a typical example of vernacular architecture is Kennixton Farmhouse from Gower, built in 1610. It was believed that its red colour protected the household from evil spirits, as did the red berries on the rowan tree.

Mae un o'r nifer o'r adeiladau a gafodd eu dwyn i Amgueddfa Werin Sain Ffagan yn enghraifft nodweddiadol o bensaernïaeth frodorol o Gŵyr a gafodd ei godi yn 1610. Y gred oedd y byddai ei liw coch yn gwarchod y preswylwyr rhag ysbrydion drwg, fel yr aeron ar y griafolen.

St Fagans
Sain Ffagan

This barn, originally from Clwyd, was built in 1550. Timber framed and made up of three parts, it suggests the old agricultural lifestyle of Wales. The largest part is made up of crucks, curved timbers reaching from the ground to the roof. Corn was unloaded and threshed through the small central doors. The straw was then stored in the building.

Daeth yr ysgubor hon o Glwyd. Cafodd ei chodi yno yn 1550. Mae ei fframwaith o goed ac yn cynnwys tair rhan sy'n awgrymu dull o fyw'r hen fywyd amaethyddol yng Nghymru. Cryciau sydd yn yr adran fwyaf, coed ardro yn estyn o'r ddaear i'r to. Câi ŷd ei ddadlwytho a'i ddyrnu trwy'r drysau bach canolog. Câi'r gwellt ei storio yn yr adeilad wedyn.

St Lythans
Llwyneliddon

It is not unusual for a mist to creep over the landscape in this part of the Vale. St Lythans, like so many of the villages west of Cardiff and south of the A48, are so close to the sea that a haar develops, and in the winter the closeness of land and sea creates many misty mornings.

Dyw hi ddim yn anghyffredin i darth gripian dros y tirwedd yn y rhan hon o'r Fro. Mae Llwyneliddon, fel cynifer o'r pentrefi i'r gorllewin o Gaerdydd ac i'r de o'r A48, mor agos at y môr fel bod llwydrew'n datblygu; ac yn y gaeaf mae agosrwydd y tir at y môr yn creu sawl bore tarthog.

Taff
Afon Taf

The River Taff rises in the Brecon Beacons and flows 36 miles to the Severn. Prone to flooding in its lower reaches, it has engulfed many important buildings, including the principal church of the city in medieval times, St Mary's, after which one of the main streets of Cardiff is named. The last major flood in Cardiff was in 1979. During the Middle Ages and until the local canals were built it was used for general river traffic, including fisherman in coracles. Today the river holds salmon, sea trout, roach, chub, dace, perch and elvers.

Mae Afon Taf yn tarddu ym Mannau Brycheiniog ac yn llifo am 36 milltir i Afon Hafren. Mae ei mannau isaf yn tueddu i orlifo ac mae wedi boddi sawl adeilad pwysig, gan gynnwys Eglwys Fair, prif eglwys y ddinas yn y canol oesoedd. Mae un o brif strydoedd Caerdydd wedi'i henwi ar ei hôl. Bu'r llifogydd mawr diwethaf yng Nghaerdydd yn 1979. Yn ystod y canol oesoedd, a than i'r camlesi lleol gael eu hadeiladu, câi ei defnyddio ar gyfer traffig cyffredinol afon, gan gynnwys pysgotwyr mewn cyryglau. Heddiw, mae ynddi eogoaid, brithyllod y môr, gwrachod, brwyniaid, draenogiaid a llysywod ifanc.

THOMAS À BECKET
THOMAS À BECKET

The marking on Thomas à Becket, the cat of the former Dean of Llandaff Cathedral, is unusual. Completely white except for his black tail he was well known for roaming the precincts of the cathedral grounds.

Mae'r marciau ar Thomas à Becket, cath Cyn-Ddeon Cadeirlan Llandaf, yn anghyffredin. Mae'n wyn i gyd, a wahân i'w chynffon ddu, ac roedd yn enwog pan oedd yn crwydro cyffiniau tir y gadeirlan.

THORNHILL
DRAENEN PEN-CRAIG

You can get a clear view of Cardiff and the Severn Estuary from the modern housing development at Thornhill.

Fe fedrwch gael golwg glir o Gaerdydd a Moryd Hafren o'r datblygiadau tai modern yn Nraenen Pen-craig.

TONGWYNLAIS
TONGWYNLAIS

The land surrounding Castell Coch is rich in trees and forests. Once part of the Butes' hunting lodge estate, today it is a favourite place for walking.

Mae'r tir o gwmpas Castell Coch yn gyfoethog ei goed a'i fforestydd. Roedd unwaith yn rhan o lety stad hela'r Teulu Bute; heddiw mae'n fan rhodio poblogaidd.

VALE OF GLAMORGAN
BRO MORGANNWG

The hedged fields of the Vale extend for miles across a soft undulating landscape.

Mae caeau perthog y Fro'n estyn am filltiroedd ar draws tirwedd esmwyth, tonnog.

VALE OF GLAMORGAN
BRO MORGANNWG

The windmill at St Y-Nyll next to the A4232 is a reminder of what used to be a common sight in the Vale until a century ago. Most villages would have had a windmill for milling corn locally, built on high ground to take advantage of the westerly winds.

Mae'r felin wynt yn Saint-y-nyll ger yr A4232'n ein hatgoffa am olygfa gyffredin yn y Fro tan ganrif yn ôl. Fe fyddai gan y rhan fwyaf o bentrefi eu melin i falu ŷd yn lleol, un wedi'i chodi ar dir uchel i fanteisio ar y gwyntoedd gorllewinol.

VICTORIA PARK
PARC VICTORIA

Opened in 1897, the park was named in honour of Queen Victoria's Diamond Jubilee. Three years later a zoological collection was started, which included a kangaroo, monkeys and storks, but its most famous occupant was Billy the Seal. When the River Ely flooded the park in 1927 he escaped from his pond and swam down Cowbridge Road.

Agorwyd Parc Victoria yn 1897 a chafodd ei enwi i anrhydeddu Jiwbilï Diemwnt y Frenhines Victoria. Dair blynedd yn ddiweddarach cychwynnwyd casgliad swolegol oedd yn cynnwys cangarŵ, mwncïod a chiconiaid, ond y preswylydd enwocaf oedd Bili'r Morlo. Pan orlifodd Afon Elái'r parc yn 1927, dihangodd o'i bwll a nofio i lawr Heol y Bont-faen.

VICTORIA PARK
PARC VICTORIA

The roof of the octagonal cast-iron fountain in Victoria Park was erected as a memorial to Lewin Samuel, who died in 1893 aged thirty-nine. In recent years it has been renovated and has changed position.

Fe gafodd to'r ffynnon wythochrog hon o haearn bwrw ym Mharc Victoria ei godi i gofio am Lewin Samuel a fu farw yn 1893 yn dri deg naw oed. Yn y blynyddoedd diweddar mae wedi cael ei adnewyddu a'i symud.

VICTORIAN
PONTCANNA
PONTCANNA
VICTORAIDD

The Victorian town housing of Pontcanna is some of the best preserved in Britain. Cathedral Road, leading to Llandaff, dates primarily from 1880–1900, with its memorable side streets named at the request of the Butes after Bishops of Llandaff – from Teilo, the first bishop, to Dogo, Berthwin, Kyveilog and Dyfrig.

Mae tai tref Victoraidd Pontcanna ymhlith y rhai sydd wedi'u cadw orau ym Mhrydain. Mae Heol y Gadeirlan sy'n arwain i Landaf yn dyddio'n bennaf o 1880–1900. Mae ganddi strydoedd ystlys cofiadwy a gafodd eu henwi ar gais y Buteiaid ar ôl Esgobion Llandaf – o Teilo, yr esgob cyntaf, at Dogo, Berthwin, Cyfeiliog a Dyfrig.

Welsh National War Memorial
Y Gofadail Genedlaethol Gymreig

The circular sunken court with Portland stone columns in Alexandra Gardens was designed by Sir Ninian Comper. In the centre the messenger of victory is encircled by leaping dolphins, which point towards the figures of a sailor, soldier and airman all lifting wreaths.

Cafodd y is-gwrt cylchog, â'i golofnau o garreg Portland, ei ddylunio gan Syr Ninian Comper. Yn y canol mae negesydd buddugoliaeth wedi'i amgylchu gan ddolffiniaid yn llamu sy'n pwyntio at ffigurau o forwr, milwr ac awyrwr, pob un yn codi plethdorch.